CAROL DOAK

# EASY reversible
# VESTS

**REVISED EDITION**

Martingale®
& COMPANY

## ACKNOWLEDGMENTS

I would like to extend my sincere thanks and appreciation to Bernina for its support and wonderful sewing machines that offer many decorative-stitch options, to Oakshott Fabrics for the delightful fabrics featured in "Plaid Garden," to Timeless Treasures Fabrics for great batiks, and to Martingale & Company for its support in making this updated version of *Easy Reversible Vests* possible.

Easy Reversible Vests, Revised Edition
© 2008 by Carol Doak

That Patchwork Place® is an imprint of Martingale & Company®.

Martingale & Company
20205 144th Ave. NE
Woodinville, WA 98072-8478 USA
www.martingale-pub.com

Printed in China
13 12 11 10 09 08          8 7 6 5 4 3 2 1

**Library of Congress Cataloging-in-Publication Data**
Library of Congress Control Number: 2008025386

ISBN: 978-1-56477-853-6

### CREDITS

President & CEO — Tom Wierzbicki
Publisher — Jane Hamada
Editorial Director — Mary V. Green
Managing Editor — Tina Cook
Technical Editor — Ursula Reikes
Copy Editor — Durby Peterson
Design Director — Stan Green
Production Manager — Regina Girard
Illustrator — Laurel Strand
Cover & Text Designer — Shelly Garrison
Photographer — Brent Kane

### MISSION STATEMENT

Dedicated to providing quality products and service to inspire creativity.

# CONTENTS

It's been more than 10 years since I wrote the best-selling book *Easy Reversible Vests*. I've traveled world-wide teaching the easy piecing techniques from that book, and my students' vests were amazingly varied. Their work inspired me to make more vests of my own. I experimented with fresh fabrics, different strip and square placements, and new block designs of varying sizes. I loved the results and was often asked if I would write an updated version of *Easy Reversible Vests*. The answer to that question is this revised edition. This book takes the best of the original *Easy Reversible Vests* and expands on it, offering even more ways to easily make flattering, one-of-a-kind vests.

The most popular styles from that book are included and described in "Vest Styles" (page 5). "Fabric and Color Selection" (page 6) has been updated with new fabric options and creative placement ideas. The tried-and-true techniques described in the first book are included, but I've also broadened the fabric suggestions and included techniques for different block placements, plus I've introduced smaller and rectangular blocks. And the section on embellishments explores different ways to decorate your vests. The "Block Designs" include the most popular designs from *Easy Reversible Vests* and expands the creative options with more designs, smaller blocks, and rectangular-block designs.

Each vest offers the opportunity to combine only strips, only squares, or both strips and squares. The patterns provide simple step-by-step instructions. With each set of project instructions, two additional vests are shown to inspire your own variations.

I'm excited to share these new vests and the easy ways to make them. I'm even more excited to see how you will embrace these ideas, add your creativity, and make them your own.

You will find full-sized patterns for the following vest styles on the pullout pattern sheets. See "Preparing the Pattern" on page 10 for more specific information on fit, seam allowances, and other details relating to using the patterns.

## STYLE A

This is a jewel-neck design with high, straight fronts that provide a large area for patchwork. On both the front and back, the lower hem curves down to a center point. Style A is the shortest of the vests, ending slightly higher at the hip than Style B.

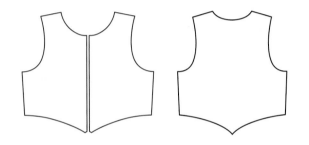

## STYLE B

This is a loose-fitting, V-neck waistcoat with pointed fronts and a straight hem at the back.

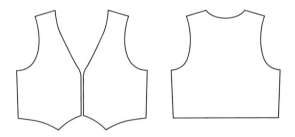

## STYLE B VARIATION

This is the same as Style B except that the back hem is double pointed, mimicking the front.

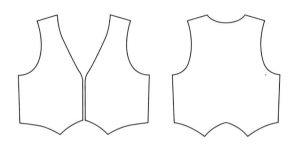

## COMMERCIAL VEST PATTERNS

You can also use an appropriate purchased vest pattern if you prefer. Look for a pattern with one back pattern piece and one front pattern piece that can be reversed for either left or right front. Do not use patterns that include darts, slip pockets, or other piecing requirements, such as fitted bodices.

Fabric and color play a huge part in the look of your vest. The fabric you choose determines whether your vest will be country, contemporary, casual, or elegant. Choose colors and fabrics that make your heart sing and that look good on you. Using favorite and flattering colors will add to the enjoyment of wearing your vests and also make others take notice.

For most of the vests in the first book, I chose a focus fabric that provided the combination of colors and overall personality of the vest. I combined varied supporting fabrics in subtle shades with a few accent fabrics to complete the overall look of the vest. In this book I expanded my approach to combining fabrics by using nontraditional quilting fabrics, fabrics with similar scale, varied scale, and varied textures, as well as fabric shading to enhance the overall look.

## FOCUS FABRICS

A focus fabric—usually a medium- or large-scale print—can make a dramatic statement and play an important part in the look of your vest. Use a focus fabric to set the theme and inspire your other fabric choices.

For the person who finds it difficult to put a group of fabrics together for patchwork, a focus fabric is a great place to start. If you choose a print because you like it, you already know you enjoy that particular mix of colors. You can confidently choose the remainder of the fabrics for the patchwork from the colors in the focus fabric. The background color of the focus fabric can be the source for the background area of the paper-pieced block. If you choose a focus fabric that has a bit of metallic gold or silver, you can add a metallic touch to your paper-pieced block.

Medium- and large-scale florals, batiks, paisleys, Asian prints, and contemporary designs make good focus fabrics. Choose prints with colors that you enjoy wearing and are passionate about.

This vest features the black focus fabric in the group of fabrics at the right. The remaining fabrics are all good focus-fabric candidates.

Fabrics with vertical stripes or linear designs are slimming and create a flattering look. Fabrics that are shaded from light to dark can also be flattering if you place the lighter portion at the top and the darker portion at the bottom. The lighter area draws the attention to the face, and the darker shades minimize the side and lower areas, making the waist appear smaller.

## SUPPORTING FABRICS

When selecting fabrics to go with your focus fabric, keep in mind that you want to choose fabrics that work as a unit, in harmony with the focus fabric rather than in competition with it. Reserve strong contrasts for small areas such as a paper-pieced block.

Tone-on-tone prints work well as supporting fabrics. Look for prints with only a slight value range, such as a medium floral design over a light background. High-contrast prints can be distracting.

Look for subtle value differences in tone-on-tone prints. These blues blend smoothly from dark to light.

These high-contrast prints don't blend well.

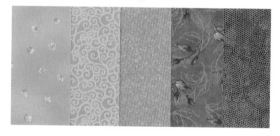

This is an effective grouping of varied prints in medium to dark fabrics featuring two colors.

## ACCENT FABRICS

Use accent fabrics to add detail or attention-grabbing design elements.

A vest in different shades of blue and purple looks stunning with yellow and gold accents.

Textures that contrast with the cottons used in the vest—such as the shine of satin or polished cotton or the subtle lines of a moiré—catch the eye and create an interesting effect.

A vest of medium-value fabrics benefits from the addition of one really dark fabric.

Fabrics that have a little metallic gold or silver in them add sparkle. If you use one of the foundation-piecing methods, you can include bits of lamé or metallic knit fabrics for a dressier look.

## CHOOSING FABRICS FOR REVERSIBLE VESTS

No matter how careful you are, the inside of a reversible vest might occasionally be visible at the vest edges. Very dark or bright fabrics can also show through if the fabrics on the other side are light. For this reason, it's best to choose similar values for the two sides of the vest. One way is to use a neutral color, such as a gray or black, with two completely different color schemes on each side of the vest. One side might be black with pink and blue, and the other side might be black with red and green.

Other than that, the possibilities are endless! One of the sides might feature satin and metallic fabrics for a dressy look, while the other side includes calicoes for a more casual look. Reversible vests can be a bonus for the traveler who likes to pack light—one piece of clothing for daytime wear with jeans that reverses to dress up a different outfit for evening.

Stripes and small-scale prints on vest backs do a great job of setting the stage for the fronts. You also have the opportunity to line the vest with just one fabric for the two fronts and another fabric for the back to make a reversible vest without patchwork.

## CHOOSING FABRICS FOR PAPER-PIECED BLOCKS

If you decide to use paper-pieced blocks in your vest, you want them to stand out from the surrounding patchwork. For this, you need contrast. An easy way to test for contrast is to select the lightest or darkest of your supporting fabrics and audition it for the background of the paper-pieced block. Does it stand out against the other fabrics in the group? If it doesn't, use an even lighter or darker fabric to get the contrast you need.

The dark background in the paper-pieced blocks in "Garden Jewel" make the flower colors pop.

## PLAYING WITH FABRIC OPTIONS

The following vests highlight the variety of ways you can play with fabrics.

**Different colors, gradated values.** For lots of color and gorgeously subtle value gradations, try combining batiks. In "Easy Dozen," batik squares blend from light yellow and pink at the top to dark brown at the bottom.

A gradation of plaids in different colors will produce a similar result, as shown in "Plaid Garden."

**Different colors, same value.** Combining several colors of the same value provides subtle variety. In "Rich Earth," I used a grouping of deep darks: black, navy, dark green, and deep purple strips run diagonally across the lower right. If you wanted a different mood, combinations of light or medium fabrics would be just as effective.

**Neutral background.** Neutrals such as black, gray, and beige make wonderful support fabrics. They are easy to blend and do not call attention to themselves. When used on the two sides of a reversible vest, they can support completely different focus fabrics. Black was used in both "Country Elegant" shown here and in "Rich Earth" at left to support different colors.

**Same color, different values.** Select several shades of the same color in varying print scales and in a range of values. For "Red Power Tie," I used strips cut from several old red ties. One-color groupings make wonderful wardrobe bridges. The different shades mean your vest will work well with other garments of the same hue.

**Watercolor gradation.** To make a watercolor-style vest, arrange floral prints in a value gradation. For this "English Garden" vest, I placed light values at the top and darker values at the bottom.

Once you have played with the possibilities and chosen your fabrics, it's time to make your vest a reality. With a little preparation and the right tools, you will be sewing in no time!

## PREPARING THE FABRIC

Prewash all washable fabrics. Press laundered fabrics to remove any wrinkles. Do not prewash specialty fabrics like velvet, silk, and satin. These are generally dry-cleaned. Use 100%-cotton fusible interfacing to stabilize delicate fabrics such as lamés and lightweight silks.

## PREPARING THE PATTERN

After choosing a vest style and size, trace the pattern pieces onto tracing paper. Tracing allows you to keep intact all the sizing and style options that are printed on the master pattern. Because it's transparent, tracing paper also makes it easier to place design elements where you want them. When transferring the patterns, label the right sides of the left and right vest fronts with a red pencil. This will alert you when you are cutting fabric for the fronts so you won't become confused!

These vest patterns include 3/8"-wide seam allowances (less bulky than the usual 5/8"). If you're using a purchased pattern that has 5/8"-wide seam allowances, simply stitch as directed and then trim the seam allowances to 3/8".

If you want to make a vest that does not button, cut the front pattern pieces 3/8" from the center-front line to allow for seam allowances.

## ENSURING A GOOD FIT

Before you begin creating your vest, it's important to check that the size and style you've selected will provide a good fit. Cut out muslin pattern pieces and baste them at the shoulders and side seams to check the fit. You don't want to go to the trouble of making your patchwork vest only to find out later that it doesn't fit as you would like.

## CUTTING THE FOUNDATION

Use 100% cotton for your foundation fabric. If most of your fabrics are dark, use a dark solid. If most of your fabrics are light, use a light-colored fabric, such as muslin.

To make the foundation, pin the pattern piece to the fabric and cut around the perimeter. To cut out two identically shaped front foundations, fold the fabric and cut both pieces at once. To cut out a back foundation, fold the fabric and place the center back of the pattern on the fold.

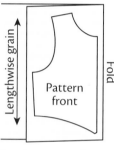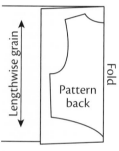

Cut the pattern front from a double layer for 2 pattern fronts.

Place the pattern back on the fold.

IMPORTANT! Mark the two front foundation pieces "left front" and "right front" so you don't make two left fronts or two right fronts by mistake. Even if you only make one front foundation, mark the right side of the fabric so you don't end up sewing strips to the wrong side.

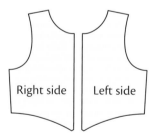

## CUTTING ONE-PIECE SECTIONS

If you're using a single piece of fabric for a vest front or back, cut these out now so that you'll have the remaining fabric available for patchwork. (See page 39 for more about one-piece sections.)

The chart below indicates the yardage needed for one-piece sections or multiple one-pieced sections from the same vest fabric or foundation fabric in the two vest styles.

| Yardage Requirements for Whole Pattern Pieces (42"-Wide Fabrics) Vest Styles A, B, and B Variation | | | | | |
|---|---|---|---|---|---|
| Size | 1 Front* | 1 Back | 2 Fronts | 1 Front and 1 Back | 2 Fronts and 1 Back |
| P | ¾ yard | ¾ yard | ¾ yard | ¾ yard | ¾ yard |
| S | ¾ yard | ¾ yard | ¾ yard | ¾ yard | ¾ yard |
| M | ¾ yard | ¾ yard | ¾ yard | ¾ yard | 1½ yards |
| L | ¾ yard | ¾ yard | ¾ yard | ¾ yard | 1½ yards |
| XL | ¾ yard | ¾ yard | ¾ yard | ¾ yard | 1½ yards |
| *"Front" refers to either a right- or left-front pattern piece.* | | | | | |

## TOOLS AND SUPPLIES

Listed below are some of the tools and supplies you'll need to make your reversible vest.

### The Basics

- Sewing machine in good working order with a walking foot
- Sewing-machine needles, size 90/14 for paper piecing and 80/12 for general sewing
- Flat-headed pins
- Rotary cutter and mat
- 3½" x 24" rotary-cutting ruler with 45°-angle markings
- 6" x 6" rotary ruler
- 6" Add-A-Quarter ruler and 6" Add-An-Eighth ruler for small pieces
- Postcard or 3" x 5" card
- Tracing paper for the paper-pieced blocks, if tracing, and for the vest patterns
- Paper for foundation piecing if photocopying the blocks
- Pressing cloth to protect delicate fabrics
- Lightweight fusible interfacing

### Optional Extras

- Sewing-machine topstitch needle for machine embroidery
- Decorative machine-embroidery thread
- Ribbons for embellishments
- ¾"-wide elastic for the back elastic
- Hera fabric marker
- Ballpoint bodkin to push out vest seams
- Chalk pencils or marker

Sewing strips of fabric, either whole or pieced, is a quick and easy way to create patchwork on the vest pattern pieces.

## CUTTING STRIPS

To cut fabric strips for foundation piecing, do the following:

1.  Fold the fabric in half with selvages matching. Then bring the long fold of the fabric up so that the fold is parallel to and just below the selvages.

2.  Position the fabric on the cutting mat with the last fold closest to you and the uneven edges on your left. (Reverse these directions if you're left-handed.)

3.  Line up one edge of a 6" square ruler even with the last fold of the fabric. Position a long ruler to the left of the square and remove the square.

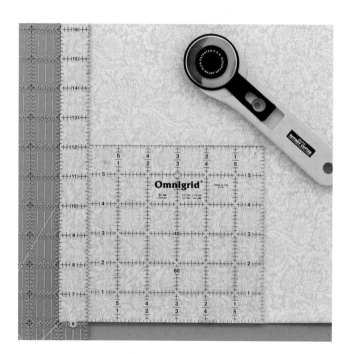

Clean cut the edge.

4.  Use a rotary cutter and cut along the right-hand edge of the ruler to make a clean cut across the width of the fabric. Cut away from yourself using firm, downward pressure. Be careful not to let the ruler slip out of position as you cut. Discard the trimmed-away fabric.

5.  Cut strips of fabric, aligning the clean-cut edge of the fabric with the ruler markings at the desired width.

Cutting strips

NOTE: Strips can be cut to a single width or in varying widths. I usually cut strips that range from 1" to 2½" wide. A design worked in 1"-wide finished strips looks quite different when worked in 2"-wide finished strips. To gauge the appearance of the finished size of the strips you intend to cut, place the rotary ruler on the fabric at the finished size. When you decide on a finished size, simply add ½" for the seam allowances to determine the cut size.

## PLACING STRIPS

You can place strips on the vest foundation vertically, horizontally, or diagonally.

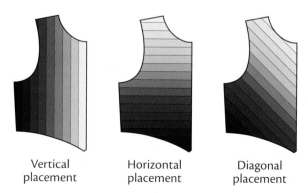

Vertical placement     Horizontal placement     Diagonal placement

Some strip placements are more figure-flattering than others.

Diagonal strips toward the center are flattering.

Diagonal strips toward the hips are not flattering.

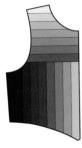

Vertical strips create a slimming effect.

Short horizontal strips flanked by vertical strips create a waist-slimming effect.

You can also change directions by orienting strips in one direction first and then adding strips in another direction. (See page 20 for instructions for adding strips in two directions.)

Sew these strips first and sew the first opposite-direction strip across the raw edges.

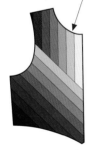

Vertical and diagonal placement

Two-way diagonal placement

Sew these strips first and sew the first diagonal strip across the raw edges.

Diagonal and vertical placement

In addition to positioning the strips in different directions to create interest and flatter the figure, you can use strip width, color, and value as design elements. Strip widths can be consistent, alternate, form a repetitive pattern, or vary randomly.

Strips all the same width

Alternating strip widths

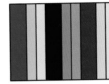

Strip widths that create a pattern

Strip widths that vary randomly

Similarly, colors can be placed in a consistent fashion, alternate, form a pattern, or vary randomly. Only one strip width is used in the example; remember that the widths can also vary, as discussed previously.

Strips all the same color

Alternating colors

Colors that form a pattern

Random colors

You can place strips of certain values for deliberate effect. Again for the sake of example, strips of the same width are depicted; widths can vary.

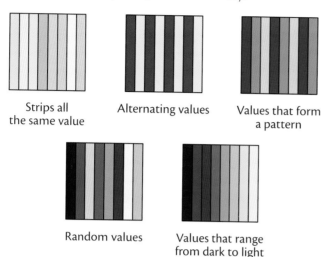

Strips all the same value

Alternating values

Values that form a pattern

Random values

Values that range from dark to light

For an organized individual, the tendency to repeat a sequence comes naturally. Placing fabric widths, colors, and values randomly is sometimes difficult. To force myself to place strips randomly, I sometimes pick up the next strip without looking and only switch if it is identical to the strip that preceded it.

## PIECED SEGMENTS

You can add interest to whole-fabric strips by inserting small pieced segments of patchwork. To break up the full-length strips with segments of patchwork, do the following:

1. Cut short segments, all the same length, from four or five of your cut strips.

2. Using a ¼"-wide seam allowance, sew the segments together as shown below.

3. Press the seam allowances in one direction.

1½"
2"
1¾"
1½"

4. Place the strip unit on the cutting mat and trim one short edge cleanly. Cut segments in the same width (or widths) as the full-length strips you are using.

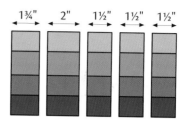

1¾"  2"  1½"  1½"  1½"

5. Sew these pieced segments randomly to the whole-fabric strips at the beginning, at the end, or in the middle; then add the pieced strips to the foundation. (See "Sewing Strips to the Foundation" on page 18.)

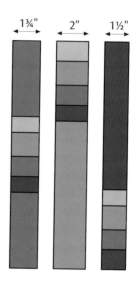

1¾"  2"  1½"

You can place the pieced segments in an organized fashion in the strip, or simply join two fabrics to create pieced strips and place them in a random or organized fashion.

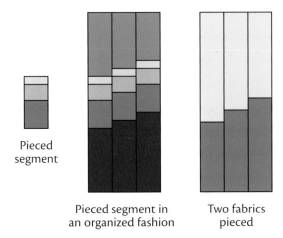

Pieced segment

Pieced segment in an organized fashion

Two fabrics pieced

## PIECED STRIPS

You can place pieced strips next to each other or alternate full-length strips of fabric with pieced strips cut vertically or diagonally. Place the pieced units with fabrics in the same position each time for a continuous look, or offset fabrics from strip to strip. Offsetting yields different results, depending on whether fabrics in the pieced strips are all the same width. Pieced sections may also be placed in a random fashion. Although the illustration shows these options using straight-cut strips placed vertically, you can do the same with horizontal and diagonal placements and diagonally cut pieced strips.

**Pieced strips of the same width**

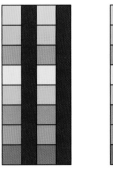

Fabric and seams are aligned.

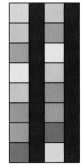

Pieced strips are offset by one fabric.

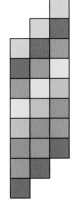

Pieced strips are offset without alternating strips.

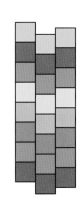

Seams are randomly placed without alternating strips.

**Pieced strips of different widths**

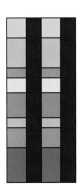

Fabric and seams are aligned.

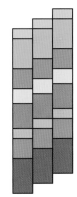

Pieced strips are offset by one fabric.

You can get another look by placing pieced strips and fabric strips diagonally on the foundation.

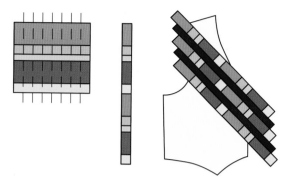

## MAKING PIECED STRIPS
### Straight-Cut Pieced Strips

1. Join several fabric strips of the same width or varying widths along the long edges.

2. Crosscut the strips at the same width and join the segments end to end until the unit is long enough to cover the foundation.

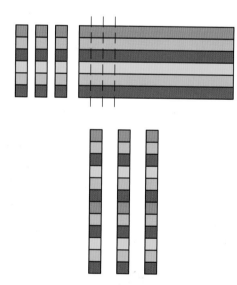

NOTE: If you want the pieced unit to form squares on the vest, use strips of uniform width to make the strip unit, and then crosscut at the same width the original strips were cut. For example, if you joined 2"-wide strips to make the strip unit, crosscut at 2" intervals.

3. Fabrics in the pieced strips can be aligned, offset, or randomly placed. After you sew a pieced strip to the foundation, trim the strip even with the foundation edge and use the remainder as needed for subsequent rows.

## Diagonally Cut Pieced Strips

1. Join several strips of fabric of the same width or varying widths along the long edges.

2. Align the 45° line on your rotary ruler with one horizontal line of the strip unit. Make the first cut diagonally across the width of the strip unit. Align the desired width on the ruler with the diagonally cut edge of the fabric and keep the 45° line along a horizontal line of the strip unit. Continue to cut subsequent segments parallel to the first cut and in the desired width by moving the ruler down the pieced strip unit.

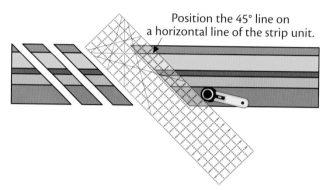

Position the 45° line on a horizontal line of the strip unit.

NOTE: Some rotary rulers show a 45° line going in both directions. Others have only one 45° line. You may need to turn the ruler over in order to place the 45° line on a horizontal seam line.

3. Join segments to create pieced strips long enough for diagonal placement on your vest.

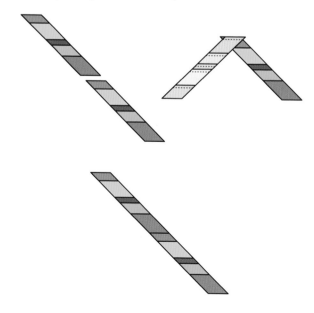

If the pieced strips are placed diagonally on the foundation in the same direction as they were cut, the seams will be horizontal. Fabrics in the pieced strips can be aligned, offset, or randomly placed.

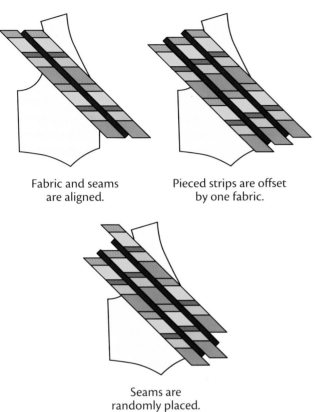

Fabric and seams are aligned.

Pieced strips are offset by one fabric.

Seams are randomly placed.

If the pieced strips are placed diagonally on the foundation in the *opposite* direction from the way they were cut, the seams will be vertical. Again, the pieced seams can be aligned, offset, or randomly placed.

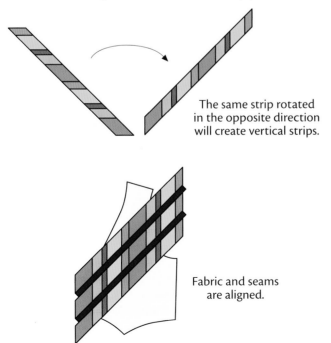

The same strip rotated in the opposite direction will create vertical strips.

Fabric and seams are aligned.

If you want to piece the vest fronts so that they are mirror images of each other, you will need to cut the pieced strips diagonally in one direction for one side and diagonally in the opposite direction for the other side. To cut strips in the opposite direction from those previously illustrated, simply place the ruler diagonally in the opposite direction and cut in the same manner.

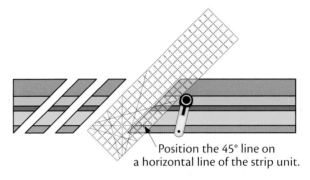

Position the 45° line on a horizontal line of the strip unit.

### RULE FOR DIAGONALLY CUT PIECED STRIPS

Pieced strips placed in the *same* direction as they are cut appear horizontal. Pieced strips placed in the *opposite* direction from the way they are cut appear vertical.

When you place diagonally cut pieced strips on the foundation vertically, still other design possibilities develop. The same options for aligning or offsetting the fabrics exist. Here again, if you want the pieced strips on the right and left fronts to mirror each other, cut them in opposite directions.

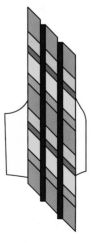

Fabric and seams are aligned.

## SEWING STRIPS TO THE FOUNDATION

Using an even-feed or walking foot attachment on your sewing machine will help you sew smoothly through many layers. These attachments feed top and bottom fabrics through the machine at the same rate, so the foundation remains flat. Let the sewing machine take the fabric—just steer the fabric strips into the needle. Don't tug on the fabric at all, because that can cause gathers or puckers.

1. Mark a vertical line (red line shown in illustration) through the center of the foundation where the edge of the first strip will be placed. If placing strips vertically, make this line parallel with the vest front edge. If placing strips diagonally, mark this line through the center of the foundation that is at a 45° angle to the vest front edge.

2. Pin the first strip right side up along the edge of the line in the center of the foundation, running either straight up and down or at a 45° angle.

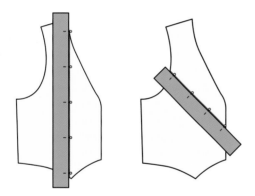

3. Check the length of the second strip by placing it right side up on the foundation alongside the center strip. Remember that ¼" along each strip will be taken up by seam allowances. It is

especially important to check the length of the strips you are sewing at an angle. You may be surprised by how much length is required.

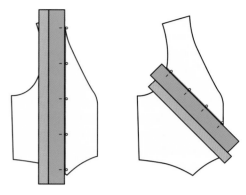

The length for the next strip is determined with the fabric right side up.

4. Place the second strip on the center strip with right sides together and raw edges even. Sew through both fabrics and the foundation, ¼" from the edge.

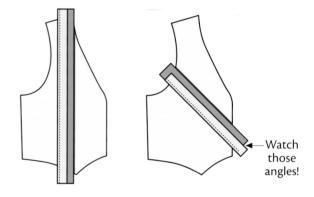

←Watch those angles!

5. Open the top strip and press with a dry iron on the cotton setting or whatever setting is appropriate for the fabrics you are using.

   CAUTION: Many specialty fabrics (lamé, metallic, knit, silk, and so on) melt at higher heat settings, so be sure to use a pressing cloth and lower the heat setting on your iron if you're using any of these fabrics in your pieced vest.

6. Continue to add strips, always checking length first, until half of the foundation is covered.

7. Return to the center and add strips to the other half of the foundation in the same manner. After all the strips have been added, trim the patchwork flush with the foundation fabric.

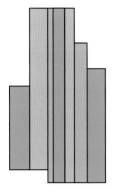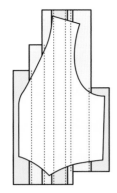

Vest front foundation with pieced strips as seen from the right side

Vest foundation as seen from the back. Trim strips flush with the foundation edge.

If you decide to align seams in successive or alternating straight-cut pieced strips, simply align the seams in each strip with the seams in the preceding pieced strips. Pin each seam in place.

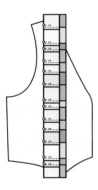

## Aligning Seams in Diagonally Cut Strips

Aligning seams in diagonally-cut pieced strips and alternating full-length strips offers more of a challenge because the seams have to line up ¼" in from the edge at the seam line.

1. Place the first pieced strip and full-length fabric strip at the desired location.

2. Place the second pieced strip, right side up, alongside the full-length strip so that the seams of the two pieced strips are approximately aligned.

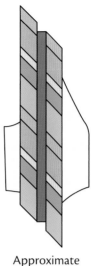

Approximate alignment of seams

3. Carefully flip the second strip over so that right sides are together, and pin in place ¼" from and parallel to the edge at the beginning, end, and in the middle. Open the strip and check that the seams match. Adjust the position of the top strip until you achieve a good match.

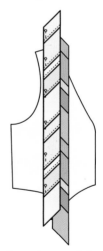

Place pins parallel to and ¼" from edge.

4. Pin in place at each seam and check one last time before sewing.

## Adding Strips in Two Directions

1. Draw a pencil line on the right-front foundation where the edges of the upper diagonal strips will be placed. This will be your stop-sewing line. It includes a ¼"-wide seam allowance.

Stop-sewing line

2. Begin with the first group of strips and foundation piece as usual. Stop sewing at the drawn line.

3. When all the strips in the first group have been sewn, pull the foundation back and trim the strips as close to the line as possible.

4. Position the first diagonal strip on the sewn strips right side up. Always overestimate. It is better to cut away excess fabric than to sew the strip and find that it's too short. Turn the strip over so that right sides are together and raw edges are even; sew ¼" from the edge.

In both vests in the following illustration, the diagonal strip that is placed on the drawn line is not pieced; however, it can be, and you can even include a paper-pieced block strip unit. See page 29.

5. Open the strip and press. Continue adding strips until the foundation is completely covered.

### MAKING MATCHING VEST FRONTS

To make two matching vest fronts using the same-strip foundation piecing, place the foundations right sides together and mark the line on the top foundation with a Hera fabric marker. This will create an identical mirrored crease mark on both foundations. Turn the top foundation over and then mark the crease lines with a pencil.

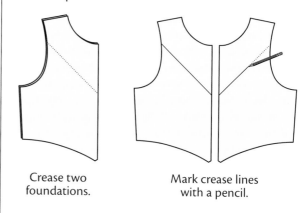

Crease two foundations.

Mark crease lines with a pencil.

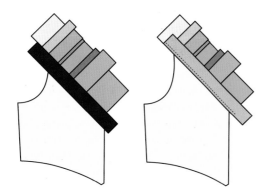

Upper diagonal strips and lower diagonal strips

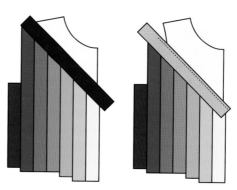

Lower vertical strips and upper diagonal strip

This technique involves sewing together squares of fabric, either whole or paper-pieced, to create a vest of squares.

When I wrote *Easy Reversible Vests*, I described a method of sewing together squares to make a pieced fabric on which the transparent vest pattern would be placed to cut the vest shape. Another method I now use is to mark a grid on the foundation the size of the finished squares and arrange the squares and/or paper-pieced blocks on the grid. I then take the squares and blocks off the foundation, sew them together in rows, and then foundation piece the rows to the foundation.

## CUTTING WHOLE SQUARES

To cut squares from a 42" strip of fabric, do the following:

1. Cut a fabric strip the width of the cut size of the square. (See "Cutting Strips" on page 12.)

2. Turn the strip and cut off the selvage and just a sliver of the fold. Line up the short end with the desired measurement on the square ruler and cut through the four layers. If you want only two squares from the strip, open the strip for two layers; if you want only one square, open it for one layer.

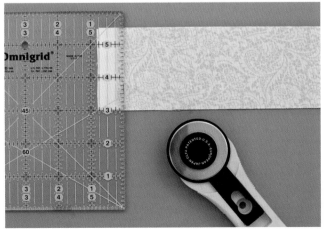

Clean cut the end.

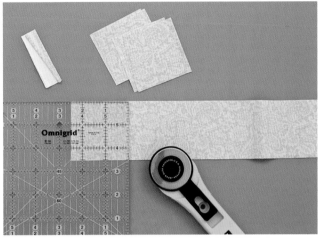

Cut squares.

3. Continue in the same manner until you have cut the desired number of squares.

## MAKING PAPER-PIECED BLOCKS

Quick and easy paper piecing offers the delightful opportunity to include intricate patchwork blocks as focal points. Paper piecing also allows you to use dress fabrics not normally used in patchwork, such as silks, satins, lamés, and metallic knits.

The vests in this book use a variety of block sizes. Some layouts require a specific block size to fit within the layout shown. Be sure to make the correct block size for the layout you are making.

### Preparation

1. Set the stitch length on the machine for approximately 18 to 20 stitches to the inch. This is the 1.5 setting on a sewing machine that has a range from 0 to 5. A short stitch length perforates the paper, so it is easier to tear away later. Use a 90/14 needle; the larger needle also helps perforate the paper. Use an open-toe presser foot for the best visibility when sewing.

2. Select sewing thread that blends with most of the fabrics used.

3. Create a pressing and cutting area next to the machine.

4. Have ready a rotary cutter, an Add-A-Quarter ruler (or Add-An-Eighth ruler if sewing small pieces), a postcard or 3" x 5" note card, and flat-headed pins.

5. Trace the block design onto tracing paper, or photocopy the design on foundation paper. Always confirm the accuracy of a photocopied paper foundation. Trim the paper foundation ½" from the solid outside line, which is also the finished seam line.

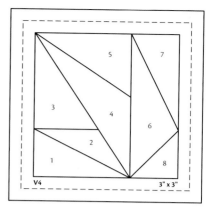

Paper-pieced design as seen from the drawing side

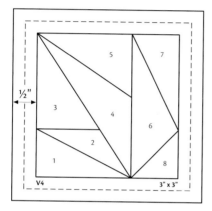

Trim the paper foundation ½" from the finished seam line.

6. Select your fabric. The unmarked side of the paper foundation is the fabric side, which means the completed block is a mirror image of the drawn block design. Note your fabric choices on the paper foundation.

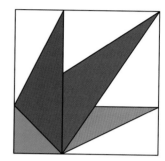

Design as seen from the completed fabric side

CAUTION: Choose nondirectional fabric for the background area of the block so that directional fabric placed along different angled seam lines will not be distracting.

7. The cutting list for each block gives the fabric size for each numbered piece. The ◻ symbol in the cutting lists indicates to cut a square the size described, and then cut the square once diagonally to create two half-square triangles. Cut the fabric pieces for the block and label them with a stick-on note indicating the number(s) where the piece(s) will be used in the block.

Although I've provided the measurements for these blocks, you may need to take new measurements should you decide to enlarge or reduce the designs. The good news about paper piecing is that the fabric pieces do not need to be an exact size. They just need to be larger than the area they are to fill. Therefore, the measuring and cutting tasks are not life-and-death issues. However, it's always better to cut too large than too small.

1. To measure for piece #1, place the rotary ruler over the area marked #1, with the ¼" line on two adjoining sides, and add at least ½" on the remaining sides to determine the new measurement. The red lines indicate the minimum size to cut.

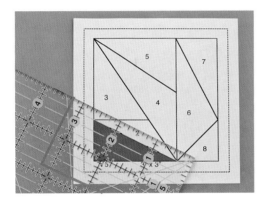

Measure piece #1.

2. To measure for the subsequent pieces, place the ¼" line of the rotary ruler on the seam line you will sew and ¼" from the end of the piece you are measuring. Let the ruler fall over the piece you are measuring. Allow for ½" extra on the opposite ends and side. The red lines indicate the minimum size to cut.

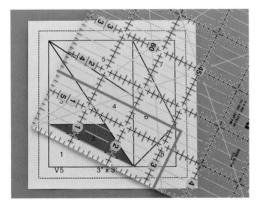

Measure the subsequent fabric pieces.

3. To measure for half-square triangle shapes, measure the short side of the triangle and add 1¼" to this measurement. Cut a square that size, and then cut it once diagonally to produce two half-square triangles.

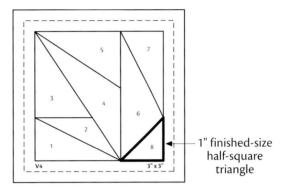

1" finished-size half-square triangle

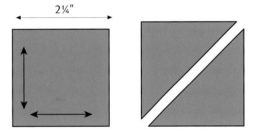

2¼"

When taking measurements for a block or just a couple of blocks, simplify the cutting tasks by cutting larger fabric sizes that will accommodate more than one area of the block. For instance, rather than cut nine different sizes of the same fabric for different areas, cut three different sizes and just use the larger fabric pieces for the smaller areas.

## Sewing

1. Using the light on your sewing machine, look through the blank side of the paper to place piece #1 right side up over the area marked #1. Turn the paper (and fabric) over and make sure the fabric covers area #1 and extends at least ¼" beyond all seam lines. Pin in place using small-headed or flat-headed pins. Place the pin parallel to the seam line between areas #1 and #2.

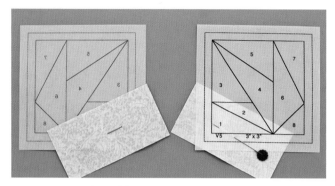

Place fabric #1 and pin in place.

2. Place the postcard on the line between areas #1 and #2, and fold the paper back to expose the excess fabric beyond the seam line.

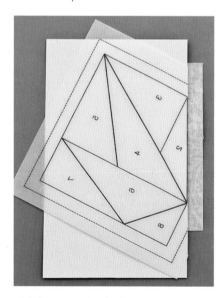

Fold the paper back along the seam line.

3. Place the Add-A-Quarter ruler on the fold and trim the excess fabric ¼" from the fold. The lip of the ruler prevents it from slipping as you trim. This trimming step produces an exact ¼" seam allowance that is parallel to the seam line. This means you will use up only ¼" of the fabric you place next to this line, and each sewn piece will open up in the same way. No surprises!

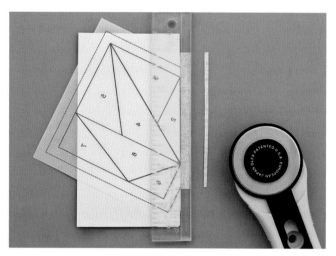

Trim piece #1.

4. Looking through the blank side of the paper to the design on the other side, place piece #2 right side up over the area marked #2. This is an important step. The reason you want to look through the blank side of the paper to position the next piece of fabric is to see how the fabric will appear after it is sewn and pressed open.

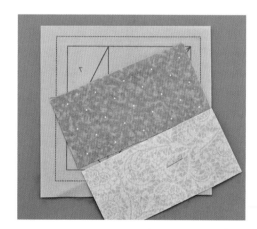

Position piece #2 over the area it will fill.

WORKING WITH SQUARES AND PAPER-PIECED BLOCKS

5. Flip piece #2 right sides together with piece #1 along the just-trimmed edge. Looking through the blank side of the paper again, check that the ends of piece #2 extend beyond *all* the seam lines of area #2 on the foundation. In the following example, I have placed red arrows to indicate the ends of the seam line for piece #2. See how the fabric has been placed to extend beyond the widest part of piece #2 to provide a seam allowance?

Flip piece #2 right sides together with piece #1.

If you are using cotton fabric, piece #2 should cling to piece #1, but if it makes you more comfortable, you can pin piece #2 in place. If you're using slippery fabrics such as satins, definitely pin piece #2 in place.

6. Place the foundation under the presser foot and sew on the seam line between areas #1 and #2, beginning about ½" before the seam line and extending the stitching ½" beyond the end of the seam.

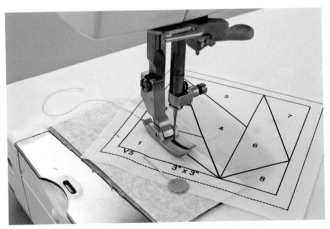

Sew the seam line between areas #1 and #2.

7. Clip the threads, remove the pin, and open piece #2. If you are using cotton fabric, press with a dry iron on the cotton setting. If you are using heat-sensitive fabric, use a pressing cloth and lower the temperature on the iron.

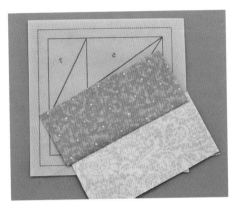

Press piece #2 open.

8. Place the postcard on the next line you will sew. This is where piece #3 adjoins the previous piece(s). Fold the paper back, exposing the excess fabric. With this seam, it will be necessary to pull the stitches away from the foundation to fold the paper, and that is okay. Place the Add-A-Quarter ruler on the fold and trim ¼" from the fold. Repeat the steps of placing the fabric right side up over the area it needs to fill and then flipping it right sides together along the seam you just trimmed. Sew on the line between areas #2 and #3, extending the stitching at each end about ½".

9. Clip the threads, open piece #3, and press. Continue in this same manner through piece #7.

Add piece #3.

10. When you are ready to sew piece #8, center the fabric triangle by aligning the point of the fabric triangle with the point of the triangle on the foundation. Sew on the line and press.

Center the triangle.

11. Using a rotary cutter and rotary ruler, align the ¼" line on the ruler on the outside solid line and trim the paper foundation and fabrics ¼" from the sewing lines on all sides.

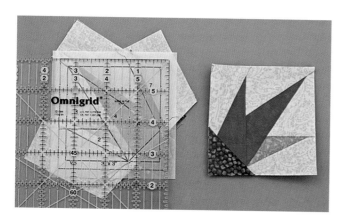

Trim the completed block.

12. Do not remove the paper yet. Keep it intact until you have sewn the paper-pieced block to the surrounding fabric pieces. When it is time to remove the paper, gently tug against the stitching to release the paper.

## PLACING AND JOINING SQUARES

Just as you do when placing strips on a foundation, you have many options for combining fabric squares or paper-pieced patchwork blocks to create vests. Squares can be joined to create a fabric, or rows of squares can be sewn to a fabric foundation. When I am incorporating paper-pieced blocks, or when I want specific placement of fabric squares, I sew the rows of squares directly on a vest foundation. With or without paper-pieced blocks, squares can be placed diagonally or vertically in a variety of ways.

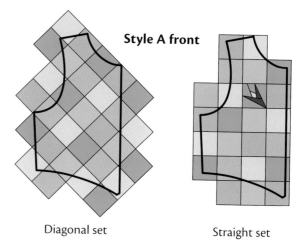

**Style A front**

Diagonal set              Straight set

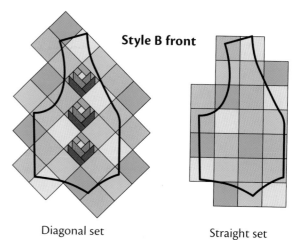

**Style B front**

Diagonal set              Straight set

WORKING WITH SQUARES AND PAPER-PIECED BLOCKS

## Joining Squares into New Fabric

1. If up to this point you have been using a pattern piece that is not transparent, make a tracing paper or tissue pattern that you can see through.

2. Place the pattern piece right side up on the table. Place your squares in the desired locations right side up on top of the pattern until the entire pattern is covered, overlapping the squares slightly to account for the ¼"-wide seam allowances.

3. Sew the squares into rows, beginning with the longest row. For each row you sew, check the length against the pattern piece and add additional squares if necessary.

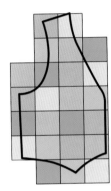

Place squares on the right side of the pattern piece to determine the approximate placement and number of rows needed.

4. Press the seam allowances in opposite directions from row to row so they will lock when the rows are joined.

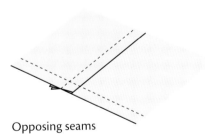

Opposing seams

5. Join rows until the sewn unit is large enough to accommodate the pattern piece. If after sewing two rows together you find that you need to add another square to the end of a row, just undo the last few stitches, add the square, and restitch.

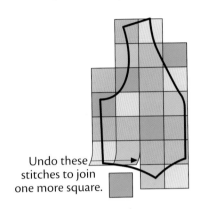

Undo these stitches to join one more square.

6. Place the transparent pattern right side up on the right side of the patchwork. Pin in place, aligning the patchwork as you would like. Cut out the pattern piece.

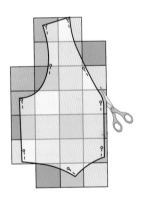

### MATCHING SQUARES ON RIGHT AND LEFT VEST FRONTS

If you want the pieced squares on both fronts to be the same, draw a pencil line on the transparent pattern front that coincides with the center seam line of the just-completed patchwork front. When you are ready to cut out the other front, position the pencil line along the same seam line.

## Sewing Rows of Squares to a Foundation

When you desire specific placement of squares, such as from dark to light, or when you want to include paper-pieced blocks at specific locations, it is easiest to use a foundation and draw the *finished-size* squares on the foundation. This allows you to position your squares exactly where they will be on the vest front and establish rows to sew.

1. To create a grid on the foundation, draw parallel vertical and horizontal lines for blocks set straight, and draw 45° diagonal lines for blocks set on point. Draw them the same distance apart as the size of the *finished* block you will be using. Place the fabric squares and/or paper-pieced blocks in the desired locations (overlapping seam allowances) to establish rows. Remove the squares from the foundation and join them in rows. Position the rows back on the foundation.

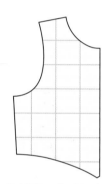
Grid lines for blocks set straight

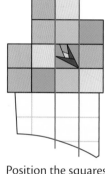
Position the squares to establish rows.

Grid lines for blocks set on the diagonal

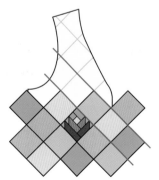
Position the squares to establish rows.

2. Carefully remove the paper from any paper-pieced blocks in the center row. Place the center row right side up on the foundation, overlapping the seam allowances along the long side of the row. Pin in place. Place the adjoining row right sides together, pin at the seam intersections, and foundation piece. Keep the paper intact in paper-pieced blocks in this second row and in subsequent rows until you sew the first seam. Once the strip is pressed open, gently remove the paper. Continue the process until the entire vest is covered with squares. Trim the excess fabric flush with the foundation.

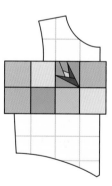

You can combine strips, squares, and paper-pieced blocks on a foundation to create even more design options.

## FRAMING PAPER-PIECED BLOCKS

One of the simplest ways to combine blocks and strips is to frame a block. Framing a paper-pieced block secures the edges of the block and makes it easier to remove the paper. You can frame a paper-pieced block with strips to make it larger, or set it with triangles to place it on point. Once the block is framed, you can remove the paper.

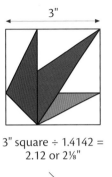

3" square ÷ 1.4142 =
2.12 or 2⅛"

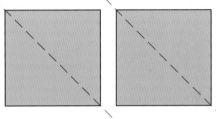

2⅛ + ⅞" (for seam allowances) = 3"

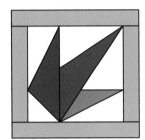

Paper-pieced block
with fabric strips

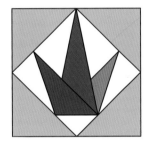

Paper-pieced block
with fabric triangles

### Framing Individual Blocks

To cut the framing triangles the correct size, including ¼"-wide seam allowances, divide the finished size of the pieced block by 1.4142 and add ⅞". Cut a square that size and cut once diagonally to make two triangles. For example, for a 3" x 3" finished paper-pieced block, 3" divided by 1.4142 equals 2.12", which is 2⅛". Add ⅞" for a total of 3". Cut two squares, 3" x 3", and cut each once diagonally to yield four corner triangles.

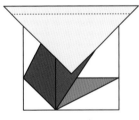 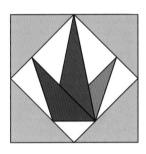

Sew the triangles to
the sides of the center square.

### Framing Blocks within a Strip

Another way to secure the edges of a paper-pieced block is to frame the block by incorporating it into the first pieced strip before you attach it to the foundation.

1.  Draw a 45° line on the foundation where the first strip will be placed. Place one or more joined paper-pieced blocks or fabric squares on the foundation in the desired location. Generously estimate the length of the fabric needed on each side of the block to cover the foundation. Be especially generous with the diagonal patchwork because the angles can be deceiving. Remove the pieces from

the foundation and sew into a strip. Position the strip back on the foundation and generously trim the ends.

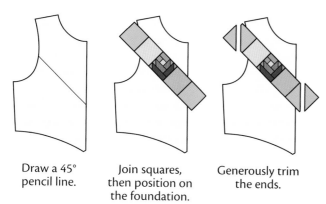

Draw a 45° pencil line.

Join squares, then position on the foundation.

Generously trim the ends.

2. You can also join a fabric strip to each side of the pieced strip. Estimate the length of the fabric strips to be added above and below. Place the strips right sides together with the pieced strip. Remove the pieces from the foundation and sew these strips to the pieced strip.

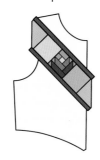

3. You can now safely remove the paper from the paper-pieced block.

4. Place the pieced strip back on the foundation, pin in place, and foundation piece above and below this pieced strip. You can add more strips, add pieced rows of squares, or add pieced rows of squares with alternating fabric strips.

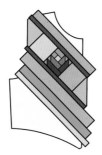

Sometimes you might want to piece your vest in a way that is not conducive to framing. It is possible to add a paper-pieced block directly to the foundation without

framing it first. Position the paper-pieced block. As you foundation piece around the block, remove the paper from the seam allowance as soon as you sew each seam. Only the paper in the center of the block will remain.

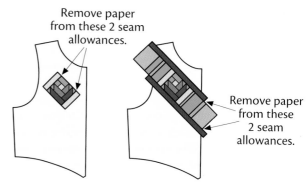

Remove paper from these 2 seam allowances.

Remove paper from these 2 seam allowances.

Once the foundation piecing is complete, carefully slit the foundation behind the paper-pieced block and remove the paper.

## PLACING STRIPS, SQUARES, AND PAPER-PIECED BLOCKS

Strips of squares, with or without paper-pieced blocks, can be placed vertically or diagonally on the foundation between alternating solid fabric strips. The following are some of the options you have for placing strips and squares in alternating rows. (For more, refer to "Pieced Strips" on page 15.)

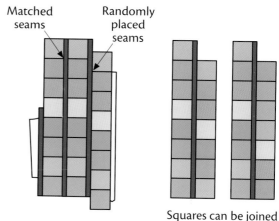

Matched seams

Randomly placed seams

Squares can be joined in the same fabric sequence or in a random fabric sequence.

You can incorporate paper-pieced patchwork blocks that are the same size as the squares. Prior to foundation piecing, attach solid fabric strips to the long sides of the pieced strip containing the paper-pieced block so you can remove the paper. (See "Framing Paper-Pieced Blocks," on page 29.)

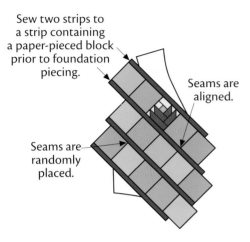

Sew two strips to a strip containing a paper-pieced block prior to foundation piecing.

Seams are aligned.

Seams are randomly placed.

Solid fabric strips can be foundation pieced around, above, or below a piece of fabric or paper-pieced block. In the illustration below, strips have been foundation pieced around a diagonally placed block, Log Cabin style.

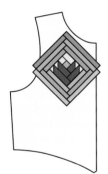

First, attach strips of fabric around the paper-pieced block and remove the paper. Then position the framed block on the foundation and foundation-piece the subsequent strips in Log Cabin fashion.

Strips can all be the same width or of various widths, as long as the strips in each row are the same width. The size of the strips can play an important part in the design as well.

You can draw parallel stop-sewing lines even with the point of the block, and foundation piece strips above and below the block. Remember to remove the paper in the seam allowances of the first round of strips. Slit

the back of the foundation to remove the paper behind the block. Foundation piece vertical strips to the left and right of the block to cover the foundation.

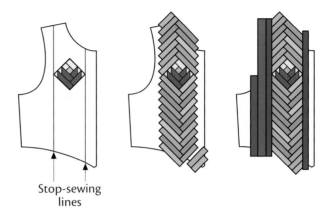

Stop-sewing lines

Just as with the other techniques, there are many design options available when you combine strips and paper-pieced blocks on a foundation. To expand those options even further, I've included some rectangular paper-pieced block designs in this book. The following is one example of a design combining a rectangular paper-pieced block and strips on a foundation.

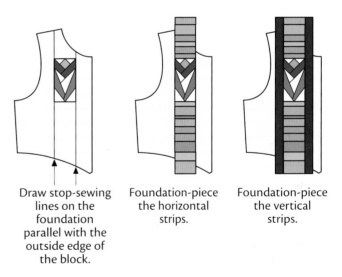

Draw stop-sewing lines on the foundation parallel with the outside edge of the block.

Foundation-piece the horizontal strips.

Foundation-piece the vertical strips.

If you forget to remove the paper or prefer to leave it on while you sew the paper-pieced block to the foundation, slit the back of the foundation to remove the paper.

Once the foundation has been completely covered with blocks, squares, and/or strips, trim the patchwork around the outside edges of the foundation.

When I wear my vests, people often notice the embellishments first. Embellishments provide that little extra touch that makes the vest special. The following are just a few ideas to consider when you want to add something distinctive to the patchwork.

## PRAIRIE POINTS

Prairie points (fabric squares folded into triangles) are quick and easy to make, and they provide delightful texture.

Prairie points on "Red Power Tie"

### Making Prairie Points

To make prairie points, cut a 2" square of fabric and fold it in one of the following ways:

1. Fold the square in half diagonally, wrong sides together, and press. Fold in half again, matching the points on the long side, and press. This method allows you to overlap points by slipping one point inside the one next to it.

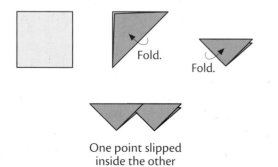

One point slipped
inside the other

2. For a center welt, fold the square wrong sides together into a rectangle, and press. Bring the corners of the long folded edge down until they meet in the center of the long cut edge. Press. Position with the center welt so it is either showing or facing down.

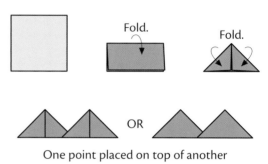

One point placed on top of another

### Sewing Prairie Points

To add a prairie point to strips being sewn to a foundation, do the following:

1. Position the raw edge of one or more points along the raw edge of the last strip you added. Baste in place 1/8" from the edge. A prairie point can be made smaller by adjusting it within the seam allowance of the strip and cutting away the excess on the long side.

The points will face toward the strips that are already in place on the foundation, so be sure to plan their placement carefully before beginning.

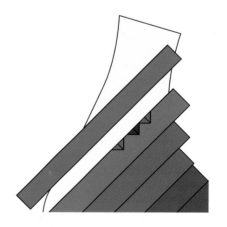

2. Sew the next strip to secure the points.

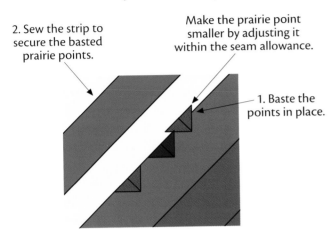

2. Sew the strip to secure the basted prairie points.

Make the prairie point smaller by adjusting it within the seam allowance.

1. Baste the points in place.

Prairie points can also be added between seamed squares or rows of squares. Machine baste the folded prairie point right side up on the right side of the square edge and stitch in place when the next square or row is joined.

Secure the tips by tacking them with a stitch. You can also add a small bead as an embellishment when you tack the points. Do this before joining two sides of the vest if you are making a reversible vest.

## DECORATIVE TOPSTITCHING

The wonderful decorative stitches available on many sewing machines are also great ways to embellish your vest. Decorative stitching can be added along seams between fabric strips or through the middle of fabric strips before the two vest sides are joined. The foundation supports the fabric and keeps it smooth as you embroider. Use a commercial tear-away paper or other piece of paper to support the fabric when you machine embroider on a single layer of fabric.

Decorative stitching on "Country Elegant"

Machine-embroidery thread is available in a wide variety of colors and fibers. Threads that contain metallic fibers offer a glittery look. Be sure to use sewing-machine needles that are designed for the type of thread you are using.

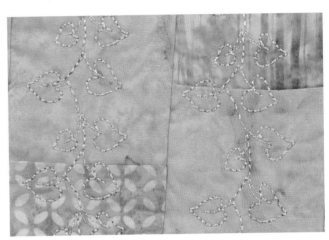

Decorative stitching with a gold metallic thread adds a bit of glitz on the upper portion of "Easy Dozen."

Test decorative stitches with the intended threads on scraps of similar fabrics first to confirm your choices. When you complete the embroidery, pull the top threads to the back by tugging on the bobbin thread at the beginning and end of the line of stitching. Tie the ends together, and then thread a needle with the tails and weave them back into the fabric.

## RIBBONS AND LACE

Embroidered ribbons, shiny ribbons, and decorative laces can add a special touch to your vest. If you sew strips to a foundation, you can use ribbons instead of fabric strips. When selecting ribbons for foundation piecing, keep in mind that if you use the sew-and-flip method, the seam allowances will take up 1/4" on each long side of the ribbon.

Another option is to topstitch the ribbon along both edges rather than sewing it into a seam. Lay the ribbon right side up, overlapping one edge of the adjoining strip, and topstitch. Join the next strip the same way. Topstitching is helpful when you don't want to lose a decorative ribbon edge or when the ribbon is heavy and would add bulk to the seam allowance. The ribbon may also be topstitched across the foundation-pieced fabrics as a decoration.

Decorative ribbon on "Streaming Blues" is topstitched to avoid losing any of the floral motif in the seams.

Ribbons and metallic threads can also be couched to the fabric. The term *couching* means simply stitching down the decorative threads or ribbons by hand or machine with another thread. These threads or ribbons can be placed in one area or scattered about the vest. They can also be placed to create flattering vertical or diagonal lines.

Strips of lace can be added in a number of ways. You can insert the lace between two strips of fabric before sewing them together. This is similar to the way in which prairie points are added; the lace will be free along one edge. Another option is to machine baste a strip of lace on top of a fabric strip of the same width and treat it as one unit. Sew lace strips and motifs onto your vest before you join the two sides of a reversible vest.

## TRINKETS, BAUBLES, AND BEADS

Small charms, bits of costume jewelry, beads, and specialty buttons can give your vest wonderful personality. Use beads as an accent or to tack down another embellishment. For instance, the pointed edges of a decorative piece of lace can be secured with beads after the lace has been stitched between two fabric strips. Be sure to add these embellishments to your vest before joining the sides.

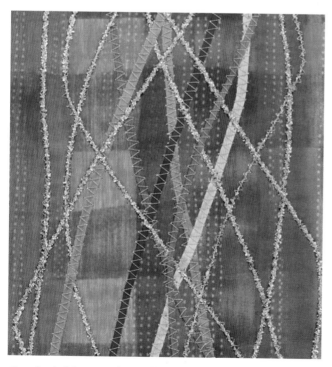

Couched ribbons and metallic threads on "Streaming Blues"

When I made my first patchwork vests using conventional methods, I felt bound to use the same patchwork technique for the right front, left front, and back. I now consider each vest section an opportunity to combine techniques and fabrics for an interesting but coordinated look. The reverse vest can have a whole new look when you keep in mind the following two considerations:

**Color.** Both sides of the vest do not need to be the same color, but the values should be somewhat similar. You are more likely to see the colors from the other side along the edges of the vest if the contrast is great. See the discussion of color on page 6.

**Foundation piecing.** If you plan on foundation piecing one of the fronts on each vest, make sure that the two pieced foundations don't end up on the same side once the vests are joined. If you're going to foundation piece the right front of one vest, foundation piece the right front of the reverse vest as well. That way each foundation is lined with a single layer of fabric and both front sections have the same weight.

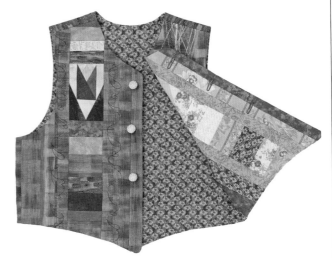

The single layer on the opposite front also backs to a foundation-pieced layer.

If you want to save time and prefer not to make two full-fledged patchwork vests for one garment, here are some ideas for making the reverse vest out of whole pieces of fabric:

- Use a pretty floral chintz, an exciting paisley, or any other fabric that appeals to you.

- Use a small-scale fabric for the back and a larger-scale coordinating fabric for the fronts.

- Use a large-scale fabric for the back and a smaller-scale coordinating fabric for the fronts.

- Use a small-scale striped fabric for the back, a larger-scale blender fabric for one front, and a coordinating small-scale print for the other front.

- When planning and making your vests, just keep in mind that they are patchwork, so there are lots of opportunities to be creative.

The single layer on the left front backs to a foundation-pieced layer.

Once you have completed two fronts and a back for each side of the vest, it's time to sew the two vests together. Use the walking-foot attachment on your sewing machine to assemble the pieces of the vest.

1. Cut interfacing pieces shown on the pattern from fusible interfacing.

2. Fuse interfacing pieces to the wrong side of the fronts on only one of the vests.

3. Fuse interfacing around the neck on only one vest back.

4. Place the two fronts of one vest on the corresponding vest back, right sides together, and pin the shoulder seams.

5. Sew with a ³⁄₈"-wide seam allowance and press the seam allowances open. Repeat with the other vest.

NOTE: If you are using a commercial pattern that has a ⁵⁄₈"-wide seam allowance, sew as directed and then trim the seam allowances to ³⁄₈".

## JOINING TWO VESTS TO MAKE THEM REVERSIBLE

1. Lay one vest on top of the other, right sides together. Pin the armholes and bottom edge of the back. Pin the bottom edge of the front, continuing up around the center front and neck edges, matching all seams. Do not pin the side openings.

2. Using a ³⁄₈"-wide seam allowance, stitch the two vests together as illustrated. Do not stitch the sides of the fronts or the back.

Do not stitch the side seams
in the front or the back!

3. Clip all curves around the neck and armholes. Cut off the points ¼" from the stitching to reduce bulk. Clip any inside angles.

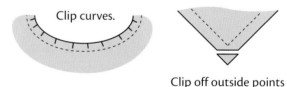

Clip curves.

Clip off outside points
¼" from stitching.

Clip inside angles.

4. Once the two vests have been joined, trimmed, and clipped, reach in from the side opening to turn the vest right side out as shown.

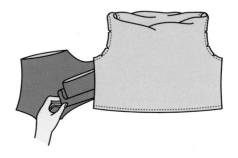

5. Use a ballpoint bodkin or a blunt tool to push out the points, and run it along the seams to push out the edges.

6. Steam press along the seams.

NOTE: If you are using heat-sensitive synthetic fabrics in your vest, use a pressing cloth and lower the iron temperature.

## SIDE SEAMS

Before you stitch the side seams, you can add elastic to the lower center back. See sidebar at right.

1. With right sides together, pin the front and back at the sides of the inside vest together between the armhole seam and the bottom seam. Follow the illustration below for pinning the seam allowances at the armhole and continue pinning to the hem.

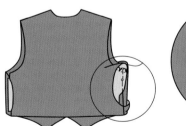
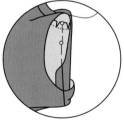

Place the seam allowances in opposite directions so they will "lock." (Side edges are shown offset so you can see the position of the seam allowances.)

2. Try the vest on to check for a good fit. Adjust the side seams if necessary.

3. Sew the side seams by machine from the bottom up, backstitching at the beginning and end. Press the seam allowances toward the back of the vest.

4. Lay the pieced section (if any) of the unsewn vest flat and overlap the single fabric side, turning under ³⁄₈". Press and blindstitch the outside seam by hand.

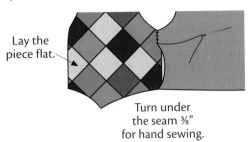

Lay the piece flat.

Turn under the seam ³⁄₈" for hand sewing.

You can add a section of elastic to the lower center back of this vest to create the illusion of a more fitted vest back.

1. Find the center back at the waistline. Lightly mark a horizontal line about 5" long. Mark another horizontal line 1" above the first line.

2. Stitch along the parallel lines through both vest backs. Use one color thread on the top and another color thread in the bobbin to match the other vest side if necessary.

3. Feed ³⁄₄"-wide elastic between the two stitching lines and stitch across one end. Pull the elastic enough to gather up the fabric slightly, and stitch the other end. Cut the elastic off about ¹⁄₂" from the end stitching lines.

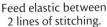

Feed elastic between 2 lines of stitching.

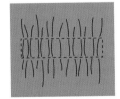

Close-up of gathered back strip

## BUTTONS

Buttons provide a wonderful opportunity for creativity. The ones you choose can add the perfect finishing touch to your original fashion vest.

Women's clothing routinely closes right over left, with the buttonholes on the right and the buttons on the left. I have found that the easiest and quickest way to use only one set of buttonholes for both vest sides is to place one set of buttonholes on the right vest front and two sets of shank-style buttons sewn back to back on the left vest front. Then the vest will button right over left on one side of the vest and left under right on the reverse side. The top buttons will be exposed on the reverse right side, giving the appearance that the vest is buttoning right over left, but it is the buttons *underneath* that are actually being used for the closure. You can, if you prefer, simply button the vest left over right on the reverse side. Consider it your magic trick!

The vest buttons right over left on this side.

The reverse side of the same vest buttons left under right.

To add buttons and buttonholes, do the following:

1. Choose a set of either three or four shank-style buttons for each vest side. Both sets should be the same size so they will function with the same buttonhole.

2. Sew the buttonholes on the right front of one patchwork vest side. You can use two different thread colors to make buttonholes. Match the top thread to the side of the vest facing up and match the bobbin thread to the vest underneath.

### CUTTING THE BUTTONHOLE OPENING

To cut the opening in machine-made buttonholes, I use a flat-edged X-acto knife rather than scissors. The knife makes a clean cut as you press down, and you don't risk snipping too far.

3. On the left front, sew a button on one side of the vest. Bring the needle through to the reverse side of the vest and slip the other button on the needle; sew it back-to-back with the first button.

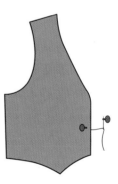

ASSEMBLY AND FINISHING

The vests presented in this section are offered as suggestions for grouping fabrics and choosing from the techniques described earlier. It is important to read all the instructional sections before making these vests. Any technique can be used in conjunction with any vest pattern. Use these vest examples as the basis for your vest or as inspiration for your own design.

Directions for each vest side include the vest pattern for the style pictured, the color, type, and amount of fabric used for one side of the vest, and information about cutting and piecing. The number of strips or squares indicated will be enough for sizes small to medium of that vest style. If you are making a larger size or different style, cut additional strips or squares from the yardage as needed.

When a vest design features a large-scale print, make a transparent pattern and move the pattern piece around on the fabric to determine the best use of the print before cutting out the pattern. For specific instructions, refer to the appropriate section for the technique you will be using. Once you have pieced your vest sides, see "Assembly and Finishing" on page 36 to complete your vest.

Yardage requirements for the fabrics used in the following vest patterns are based on 42"-wide fabric, except for specialty fabrics such as Japanese yukata. Yardage requirements for one-piece sections are not very flexible. They depend on the size and style of your vest. I cut one-piece sections on the lengthwise grain of the fabric so that the slight stretch in the crosswise grain falls on the width of the garment. The chart on page 11 gives the amount you need for any one-piece section for the three vest styles in this book. To calculate the amount you need for a purchased vest pattern, measure the pattern from shoulder to hem, including seam allowances, and buy enough fabric to accommodate the pattern piece lengthwise.

The yardage requirements for pieced sections are not as strict. They only provide an estimate of the number of fabrics needed and their relative amounts. I call for 1/8 yard of many fabrics because that is the minimum cut most stores will make. If you already have some fabric on hand, you can probably get by with less in the smaller vest size. I do call for scraps when just a tiny amount of fabric is needed, as for paper-pieced blocks. Use more or fewer fabrics than indicated, according to your preference and the yardage available to you. You have flexibility.

Many of the vests call for strips cut from the fabrics that remain after one-piece sections are cut. If you're making a large vest, you may need to cut more short strips and piece them. If you want to use a certain piece of fabric and it's not large enough for the pattern piece, feel free to join additional fabrics to it. These are patchwork vests, after all!

## VEST FACTS

### Vest Style B Variation: Combining Strips, Squares, and Paper-Pieced Blocks

Instructions on page 29.

Batik fabrics are perfect for this vest because many include a range of colors that flow from one to another. I selected a batik for the left front and gathered a group of coordinating batiks for the patchwork squares on the right front. A darker purple batik was used to create the flattering diagonal strip between the pieced squares. The paper-pieced block features lighter shade scraps against the medium blue.

## MATERIALS FOR ONE VEST SIDE

*Yardage is based on 42"-wide fabric.*

**Back:** ¾ yard of light lavender striped batik

**Foundation:** ¾ yard of light cotton fabric (1 front)

**Right Front:**

- ⅛ yard *each* of coordinating batiks in medium blue, medium teal, light blue, and pink
- ⅛ yard of dark purple batik for alternating strips

**Left Front:** ¾ yard of multicolored batik

**Paper-Pieced Block:** Medium blue batik for background, and pink, purple, and lavender fabric scraps for rays

## CUTTING AND PIECING

Cut additional squares and strips as needed if you are making a larger size or different style.

1.  From the light lavender striped batik, cut out the back.

2.  From the light cotton fabric, cut out the right-front foundation.

3.  From the multicolored batik, cut out the left front.

4.  Using the pattern on page 67, paper piece one V1 block, 3" x 3" finished.

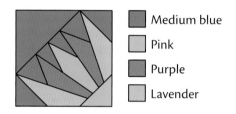

Medium blue
Pink
Purple
Lavender

5.  From the multicolored batik, the back fabric, and the four coordinating batiks, cut a total of 20 squares, 3½" x 3½". From the dark purple batik, cut two strips, 1½" x 42".

6.  Mark a 45° line on the right-front foundation where the bottom of the first row of squares, containing the paper-pieced block, will be placed (see page 30). Position the paper-pieced block and the lighter batik squares on either side. Join the squares in a row off of the foundation. Place the pieced unit on the foundation to generously estimate the length of the 1½"-wide dark purple strips above and below the unit. Cut the pieces and join them off of the foundation. Remove the paper and position the unit back on the foundation.

7.  Continue to lay out alternating rows of squares (placing the lighter ones toward the top and center of the vest) and dark purple strips. Join the squares into rows off of the foundation, and foundation piece the pieced strips to the foundation, alternating with the dark purple strips.

8.  For "Assembly and Finishing," see page 36.

BATIK BEAUTY. The beautiful multicolored batik fabric on the left front inspired the similar-colored batik squares on the right front.

BLACK TIE. The print on the right front actually mimicked a pieced front, inspiring the alternating squares and strip-pieced left front.

RED HOT. The subtle, elegant red silk fabric on the left front inspired the combination of red and black cotton prints on the right front. Prairie points add a touch of detail along the neck.

## Vest Style B Variation: Combining Strips, Squares, and Paper-Pieced Blocks

Instructions on page 29.

I selected four pastel floral fabrics featuring different scales of flowers with varying amounts of background area to create a gradual range of value from light at the top to dark at the bottom. The paper-pieced floral block features solid-colored fabrics against a white background. The light green print creates a nice diagonal line on both vest fronts.

## MATERIALS FOR ONE VEST SIDE

*Yardage is based on 42"-wide fabric.*

**Back (and Alternating Strips for Right and Left Fronts):** ¾ yard of light green print

**Foundation:** ¾ yard of light cotton fabric (2 fronts)

**Right and Left Fronts:** ⅛ yard *each* of 4 pastel floral fabrics with similar background color, featuring small- to large-scale flowers

**Paper-Pieced Block:** White fabric scrap for background, and assorted solid-colored pastel fabric scraps for flower

## CUTTING AND PIECING

Cut additional squares and strips as needed if you are making a larger size or different style.

1. From the light green print, cut out the back.

2. From the light cotton fabric, cut out two front foundations.

3. Using the pattern on page 67, paper piece one V2 block, 3" x 3" finished.

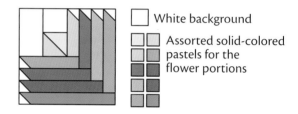

☐ White background

Assorted solid-colored pastels for the flower portions

4. From *each* of the four pastel floral fabrics, cut 12 squares, 3½" x 3½" (48 total). From the light green print used for the back, cut four strips, 1½" x 27". Be sure to cut your vest back from this yardage prior to cutting these strips!

5. Place both vest-front foundations right sides together and mark a 45° line where the bottom of the first row of squares containing the paper-pieced block will be placed (see pages 28 and 30). Position the paper-pieced block on the right-front line and the lighter floral fabric squares on either side. Join the squares in a row off of the foundation. Place the pieced unit on the foundation to generously estimate the length of the 1½"-wide light green strip above and below the unit. Cut the pieces and join them off of the foundation. Remove the remaining paper and position the unit back on the foundation.

6. Continue to lay out alternating rows of squares (placing the lighter ones toward the top and center of the vest) and light green strips. Join the squares into rows and foundation piece them to the foundation, alternating with light green strips.

7. Complete the left front in the same manner, but without the paper-pieced block.

8. For "Assembly and Finishing," see page 36.

ENGLISH GARDEN. Squares of pastel floral fabrics in varying scales and ranging slightly in value create a flattering vest that would be comfortable in any garden.

MIDNIGHT GARDEN. Even I was surprised at how this group of floral fabrics with a black background and alternating black strips worked to create such a gorgeous vest.

SET IN GOLD. This vest features textured metallic-weave fabric squares and paper-pieced blocks set in a diagonal line on both fronts.

### Vest Style B Variation:
#### Working with Squares and Paper-Pieced Blocks

Instructions on page 21.

Finished 2" squares are placed on the diagonal for both vest fronts. The squares of similar jewel-tone colors on a black background are the perfect setting to showcase three paper-pieced blocks in a vertical line on the right front.

## MATERIALS FOR ONE VEST SIDE

*Yardage is based on 42"-wide fabric.*

**Back:** ¾ yard of black-and-green print

**Foundation:** ¾ yard of black cotton fabric (2 vest fronts)

**Right and Left Fronts:** ¼ yard *each* of 6 small- to medium-scale prints featuring jewel-tone colors on black background

**Paper-Pieced Blocks:** ⅛ yard of solid black fabric for background, and solid jewel-tone fabric scraps for flowers

## CUTTING AND PIECING

Cut additional squares and strips as needed if you're making a larger size or different style.

1. From the ¾ yard of black-and-green print, cut out the back.

2. From the ¾ yard of black cotton fabric, cut out two front foundations.

3. Using the pattern on pages 60, 61, and 63, paper piece one each of blocks F1, F3, and F7, 2" x 2" finished.

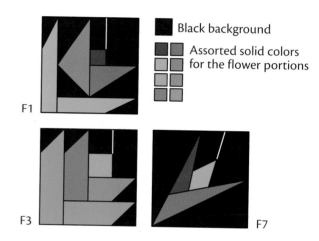

■ Black background

Assorted solid colors for the flower portions

F1

F3

F7

4. From *each* ¼ yard of six small- to medium-scale prints, cut 17 squares, 2½" x 2½" (102 total).

5. Place both vest-front foundations right sides together and mark 45° lines in both directions, 2" apart, to create 2" squares (see page 28). Position the paper-pieced blocks on the marked squares on the right front so they are positioned vertically, one beneath another as shown in the photo, and fill in with fabric squares. Join the squares in diagonal rows off of the foundation. Place the first row containing the paper-pieced block right side up on the foundation along the line overlapping the seam allowance. Position the next row above or below the first row, right sides together with seams matching; foundation piece and press open. Remove the paper in the seam allowance. Join the remaining rows in the same manner until the foundation is covered. Slit the area behind the paper-pieced block and remove the remaining paper (see page 30).

6. Complete the left front in the same manner, but without the paper-pieced blocks.

7. For "Assembly and Finishing," see page 36.

PETITE FLORALS. A variety of small- to medium-scale prints with a black background are combined with floral paper-pieced blocks to produce a versatile vest.

NEUTRALS GONE WILD. This vest features the small diagonally placed paper-pieced blocks and squares on the right front and a Japanese yukata fabric on the left.

DONNA'S GARDEN. This dramatic watercolor vest features 1½" finished floral squares ranging from light at the top to dark at the bottom.

## VEST FACTS

### Vest Style B Variation:
#### Working with Squares and Paper-Pieced Blocks

Instructions on page 21.

This wonderful collection of primary-colored plaids and stripes became the inspirational setting for three paper-pieced blocks set on point in a row near the bottom of each vest front. A solid beige is used for the background area of the paper-pieced blocks, and plaids and stripes for the design elements.

## MATERIALS FOR ONE VEST SIDE

*Yardage is based on 42"-wide fabric.*

**Back:** ¾ yard of dark red narrow-striped fabric

**Foundation:** ¾ yard of light cotton fabric (2 fronts)

**Right and Left Fronts:**

- Approximately ½ yard *total* of assorted plaid and striped fabrics ranging in colors from yellow to red, orange, burgundy, blue, and green
- ⅛ yard of dark red fabric
- ⅛ yard of dark orange fabric

**Paper-Pieced Blocks:** ¼ yard of beige fabric for background, and plaid and striped fabric scraps for design elements

## CUTTING AND PIECING

Cut additional squares as needed if you are making a larger size or different style.

1. From the red narrow-striped fabric, cut out the back.

2. From the light cotton fabric, cut out two front foundations.

3. From the assorted plaid and striped fabrics, cut 65 squares, 3" x 3". From the dark red fabric, cut 10 squares, 3" x 3", and from the dark orange fabric, cut 6 squares, 3" x 3".

4. Using the pattern on pages 70 and 72, paper piece four V5 blocks and two V9 blocks as shown, 2½" x 2½" finished.

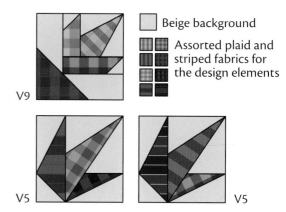

5. Place both vest-front foundations right sides together and mark 45° lines in both directions, 2½" apart, to create 2½" squares (see page 28). Mark the lines so that three paper-pieced blocks will fit centered at the lower portion of each front.

6. Position the paper-pieced blocks and fabric squares on the right front as shown in the photo. Join the squares in rows off of the foundation. Place the rows back on the foundation in the proper location. Pin the center row in place, letting the seam allowances overlap the lines. Position the next row above or below the first row, right sides together with seams matching; foundation piece and press open. Remove the paper in the seam allowance. Slit the area behind the paper-pieced block and remove the paper (see page 30). Join the remaining strips in the same manner until the foundation is covered.

7. Complete the left front in the same manner.

8. For "Assembly and Finishing," see page 36.

PLAID GARDEN. This festive vest features plaid and striped fabric squares ranging from bright-colored at the top to darker and more subtle at the bottom.

GARDEN JEWELS. Floral fabrics in varying scales positioned at the top of this vest complement the jewel-tone garden at the base.

SUMMER SCENE. Fabric squares, shading from light blue sky at the top of the vest to teals and finally to green, set the scene for the flowers growing in this garden.

## VEST FACTS

**Vest Style A:** Combining Strips, Squares, and Paper-Pieced Blocks

Instructions on page 29.

The dark rich batik on the left front was the inspiration for combining the browns, red, purple, teal, and black fabric on the right front. Lighter values of these colors are featured in the paper-pieced block. Combining a focus fabric for one vest front with a paper-pieced block and diagonal strips for the other vest front is a quick and easy way to make a stunning vest.

## MATERIALS FOR ONE VEST SIDE

*Yardage is based on 42"-wide fabric.*

**Back:** ¾ yard of dark batik A

**Left Front:** ¾ yard of dark batik B

**Foundation:** ¾ yard of dark cotton fabric (1 front)

**Right Front:** ⅛ yard *each* of black fabric and dark brown fabric, and ⅛ yard each of 6 coordinating batiks for strips

**Paper-Pieced Block:** Black fabric from right front for background, and peach, rust, and lavender fabric scraps for design elements

## CUTTING AND PIECING

Cut additional strips as needed if you are making a larger size or different style.

1. From dark batik A, cut out the back.

2. From the dark cotton fabric, cut out the right-front foundation.

3. From dark batik B for the left front, cut out the left front.

4. Using the pattern on page 71, paper piece one V7 block, 3" x 3" finished.

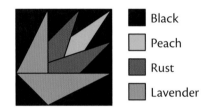

| | |
|---|---|
| ■ | Black |
| ▨ | Peach |
| ▧ | Rust |
| ▦ | Lavender |

5. From dark batik B, cut one strip, 1½" x 42". From the dark brown fabric, cut one strip, 3½" x 42". From *each* of the six coordinating batiks and the black fabric, cut 42"-long strips in widths ranging from 1½" to 1¾".

6. Mark a 45° line on the right-front foundation where the bottom of the paper-pieced block will be placed. Position the paper-pieced block and place the dark brown fabric on either side of the block to generously estimate how much is needed to complete the strip. Cut the pieces and join them off of the foundation. Place the pieced unit on the foundation to generously estimate the length of the focus-fabric strips above and below the unit. Cut the strips and join them off of the foundation. Remove the remaining paper and position the unit back on the foundation.

7. Foundation piece the remaining strips above and below this unit, placing the lighter strips toward the top and the darker strips toward the bottom.

8. For "Assembly and Finishing," see page 36.

RICH EARTH. The mouthwatering batik featuring earth-toned colors inspired the batik strips placed on the right side. The paper-pieced block features lighter batiks to create a dramatic focus.

COUNTRY ELEGANT. The large-scale painted floral fabric inspired the colors used in the radiating paper-pieced block that is set into the diagonal strip.

RED POWER TIE. The vest fronts are made completely from strips cut from old ties. The back was also foundation pieced with vertical strips cut from navy blue ties.

## VEST FACTS

### Vest Style B Variation: Combining Strips, Squares, and Paper-Pieced Blocks

Instructions on page 29.

The focus fabric containing blue lines and a yellow-and-green accent inspired not only the yellows and greens in the paper-pieced block but also the blue batik on the back and in the paper-pieced block strip. The vertical lines of the focus fabric are enhanced with a few vertical machine-embroidered lines on the left front, and one diagonal line on the right front.

## MATERIALS FOR ONE VEST SIDE

*Yardage is based on 42"-wide fabric.*

**Back (and Paper-Pieced Block Background):** ¾ yard of blue batik

**Foundation:** ¾ yard of light cotton fabric (1 front)

**Right and Left Fronts:** ¾ yard of blue linear focus fabric

**Paper-Pieced Block:** Blue batik (from the back), yellow, light green, and medium green fabric scraps for design elements

## CUTTING AND PIECING

Cut additional strips as needed if you are making a larger size or different style.

1. From the blue batik, cut out the back.

2. From the light cotton fabric, cut out the right-front foundation.

3. From the blue focus fabric, cut out the left front.

4. Using the pattern on page 75, paper piece one rectangular V13 block, 3" x 6" finished.

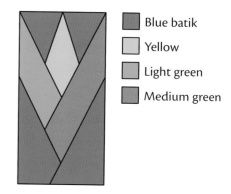

| | |
|---|---|
| ■ | Blue batik |
| □ | Yellow |
| ▨ | Light green |
| ▦ | Medium green |

5. If the stripes on the focus fabric run horizontally from selvage to selvage, cut two strips, 2" x 42", and two strips, 1½" x 42". If the stripes on the focus fabric run parallel with the selvages, cut three strips, 2" x 27", and three strips, 1½" x 27". From the remaining blue batik back fabric, cut one strip, 3½" x 27".

6. Mark a 45° line on the right-front foundation where the strip unit containing the paper-pieced rectangular block will be placed (see page 20). Mark a vertical line in the middle of the lower section parallel to the right-front edge as a guideline for the first vertical strip. Place a 2"-wide focus-fabric strip right side up along this vertical line. Foundation piece 1½"-wide focus-fabric strips on each side and press open. Use the 45° line as the guide for the top edge of each strip. Continue to foundation piece, alternating strip widths until the lower portion of the vest foundation is covered. Fold the foundation back along the pencil line and trim the vertical strips close to the line (see page 20).

7. Mark a parallel 45° line on the foundation 1¼" above the first pencil line as your guide for the strip containing the paper-pieced block. Place the block along this marked line. Position a 3½"-wide strip of the blue batik on each side to generously estimate how much is needed to complete the strip. Cut the

pieces and join them off of the foundation. Place the pieced unit on the foundation to generously estimate the length of the 1½"-wide focus-fabric strips above and below the unit. Cut the strips and join them off of the foundation. Remove the remaining paper.

8. Place the strip unit along the 45° line, right sides together with the vertical strips. Pin in place ¼" along the edge and open the strip to test that it will cover the foundation. Foundation piece and press open. Continue to foundation piece strips of focus fabric to cover the remaining upper portion of the foundation. Slit the area behind the paper-pieced block and remove the remaining paper (see page 30).

9. If desired, add vertical lines of decorative machine stitching on the left front and a diagonal line on the upper strip in the right front.

10. For "Assembly and Finishing," see page 36.

TROPICAL BLUES. The bright blue linear fabric with the green and yellow accents on the left front inspired the fabrics on the right front.

SPRING HAS SPRUNG. The dramatic floral striped fabric in the upper portion of the vest was the inspiration for the vertically pieced green and beige strips used on both fronts and on the vest back.

OUT OF THE FIRE. The elegant silk fabric that shades from black to gold to red inspired the vertical and diagonal placement of the strips on the right front.

## VEST FACTS

**Vest Style A:** Combining Strips, Squares, and Paper-Pieced Blocks

Instructions on page 29.

A lovely large-scale focus fabric is used on the left front. The right front features a rectangular paper-pieced block set vertically and foundation pieced with short strips of focus fabric and similar-colored scraps above and below the block. Pink vertical strips are foundation pieced along each long side first, focus fabric strips, and the remaining strips are the light and medium teal fabrics.

## MATERIALS FOR ONE VEST SIDE

*Yardage is based on 42"-wide fabric.*

**Back:** ¾ yard of medium teal fabric

**Foundation:** ¾ yard of light cotton fabric (1 front)

**Right Front:** ⅛ yard of medium pink fabric, ⅛ yard of light teal fabric, and fabric scraps of light blue, teal, and pink for short horizontal strips

**Left Front:** ¾ of yard large-scale print

**Paper-Pieced Block:** Muslin for background, and yellow, light pink, medium pink, light green, and medium green fabric scraps for flower

## CUTTING AND PIECING

Cut additional strips as needed if you are making a larger size or different style.

1. From the medium teal, cut out the back

2. From the light cotton fabric, cut out the right-front foundation.

3. From the large-scale print, cut out the left front.

4. Using the pattern on page 77 and the fabric scraps, paper piece one V15 block, 3" x 6" finished.

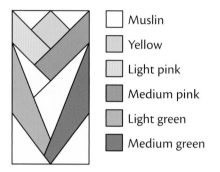

☐ Muslin
☐ Yellow
☐ Light pink
☐ Medium pink
☐ Light green
☐ Medium green

5. From the medium pink fabric, cut one strip, 1¼" x 42". From *each* of the remaining large-scale print and the medium teal fabric for the back, cut one strip, 2½" x 42". From the light teal fabric, cut one strip, 2" x 42". From the large-scale print, the back fabric, and the assorted light blue, teal, and pink fabrics, cut a total of 10 pieces, 3½" long, and in widths ranging from 2" to 2½".

6. Mark two parallel pencil lines in the center of the right foundation, 3½" apart (see page 31). Center the paper-pieced block in the upper portion between the lines. Foundation piece the 3½"-long strips above and below the paper-pieced block. Remove the paper in the seam allowances. Continue until the entire area between the lines is covered.

7. Place the medium pink strips along the long edge, right sides together. Pin in place, foundation piece, remove the paper in the seam allowance, and press open. Add the focus-fabric strips next, and then the light and medium teal strips until the foundation is covered. Slit the area behind the paper-pieced block and remove the remaining paper (see page 30).

8. For "Assembly and Finishing," see page 36.

GARDEN PARTY. The large-scale print on the left front reminded me of lovely vintage tablecloths. The gorgeous soft flowers set in the large striped area inspired the paper-pieced block in the pieced strip on the right front.

STREAMING BLUES. The blue fabric used on the left front is embellished with couched metallic thread and ribbon. The right front features a paper-pieced rectangular flower block and a gold embroidered ribbon.

ASIAN BRONZE. A collection of Asian prints ranging from dark brown to a light bronze is used as vertical strips on the right front. The left front features a pieced strip with two rectangular paper-pieced blocks set vertically with short strips.

### Vest Style A: Combining Strips, Squares, and Paper-Pieced Blocks

Instructions on page 29.

The floral-and-striped focus fabric used on the left front inspired the paper-pieced flower block worked in yellows against a blue background. The short strips include the focus fabric, the back fabric, and a few additional blue and yellow fabric scraps. The vertical strips include a few additional blue fabrics.

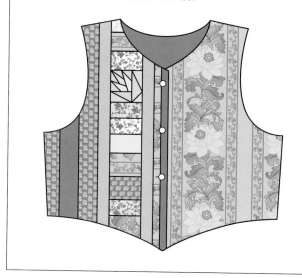

## MATERIALS FOR ONE VEST SIDE

*Yardage is based on 42"-wide fabric.*

**Back:** ¾ yard of blue-and-yellow print

**Foundation:** ¾ yard of light cotton fabric (1 front)

**Right Front:**

- ⅛ yard *each* of light blue, medium blue, and medium dark blue fabrics

- 4 assorted fabric scraps for short horizontal strips

**Left Front:** ¾ yard of large-scale blue-and-yellow striped fabric

**Paper-Pieced Block:** Light blue fabric for background area, and assorted light and medium yellow fabric scraps for design elements

## CUTTING AND PIECING

Cut additional strips as needed if you are making a larger size or different style.

1. From the blue-and-yellow print, cut out the back.

2. From the light cotton fabric, cut out the right-front foundation.

3. From the large-scale blue-and-yellow striped fabric, cut out the left front.

4. Using the pattern on page 71, paper piece one V7 block, 3" x 3" finished.

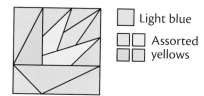

Light blue

Assorted yellows

5. From the medium blue fabric and left-front focus fabric, cut one strip each, 1½" x 42". From the back fabric and medium dark blue fabric, cut one strip *each*, 2" x 42". From the four assorted scrap fabrics, the focus fabric, and the back fabric, cut a total of 10 pieces, 3½" long, in widths ranging from 2" to 2½".

6. Mark two parallel pencil lines in the center of the right foundation, 3½" apart (see page 31). Center the paper-pieced block in the upper portion between the lines. Foundation piece the 3½"-long strips above and below the paper-pieced block. Remove the paper in the seam allowances. Continue until the entire area between the lines is covered.

7. Place the medium blue fabric strips along the long edge, right sides together. Pin in place, foundation piece, remove the paper in the seam allowances, and press open. Add the focus-fabric strip to the right, and add the back fabric to the left. Add the medium dark blue fabric to the right and the left. Continue to alternate between the back fabric and medium dark blue fabric on the left until the foundation is covered. Slit the area behind the paper-pieced block and remove the remaining paper (see page 30).

8. For "Assembly and Finishing," see page 36.

BUTTERCUP. Blue and yellow is always a happy combination. The large-scale floral-and-striped fabric on the left front inspired the horizontal and vertical strips on the right front.

JAPANESE SAMPLER. The Japanese sampling of floral prints on the left front inspired the radiating paper-pieced block design set into the right front with horizontal and vertical strips.

ORIENT EXPRESS. This vest features a focus fabric of horizontal and vertical floral prints on the right front. The left front continues the theme in shades of blue and orange.

## VEST FACTS

### Vest Style B Variation: Working with Strips

Instructions on page 12.

This vest begins with a great multicolored batik focus fabric used on the back. Twelve textured batiks (hence the name of this vest), ranging from light to dark values in the colors featured in the focus batik, are pieced in a strip set. Segments are cut and foundation pieced in stair-step fashion, with the darker shades placed in the lower portion of the vest fronts. A bit of gold embroidery enhances the upper portions.

## MATERIALS FOR ONE VEST SIDE

*Yardage is based on 42"-wide fabric.*

**Back:** ¾ yard of multicolored batik focus fabric

**Foundation:** ¾ yard of light cotton fabric (2 fronts)

**Right and Left Front:** ⅛ yard *each* of 12 batiks, ranging from light to dark, in colors of multicolored batik focus fabric used on back

## CUTTING AND PIECING

Cut additional strips as needed if you are making a larger size or different style.

1.  From the multicolored batik focus fabric, cut out the back

2.  From the light cotton fabric, cut out two front foundations.

3.  From *each* of the 12 batiks, cut one strip, 2½" x 42". Sew the strips together along the long edges and press the seam allowances toward the darker fabric strip. Clean cut one end and cut 14 segments, 2½" wide. Cut additional segments as needed. See "Making Pieced Strips" on page 16.

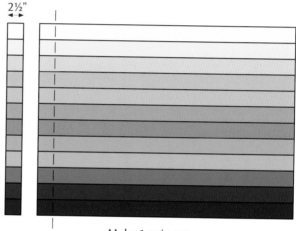

2½"

Make 1 strip set.
Cut 14 segments.

4.  Mark two vertical lines, 2½" apart, on the right- and left-front foundations, starting 3" from the front edges and parallel to the front edge. Place the first strip set right side up between the lines, with the lightest square just covering the top of the foundation. Place the subsequent strips right sides together, offset by half of a block toward the top of the vest; foundation piece and press. Continue until the entire foundation is covered.

5.  Embellish with machine-embroidered stitching in the upper area of the vest. See page 33.

6.  For "Assembly and Finishing," see page 36.

EASY DOZEN. The vest takes advantage of the great range and flowing colors in batik fabrics. Darker colors in the lower portion and lighter colors in the upper portion provide a flattering image.

SIMPLY A GARDEN. Light to dark floral fabrics are strip pieced and offset by half of a block to create this flattering watercolor-style garden.

JUST PLAIN FUN! The playful large-scale floral inspired this color combination. Pieced strips are offset between the focus fabric and the black.

The following paper-pieced designs feature varied sizes and styles, offering lots of creative opportunities. I have repeated a few of the tried-and-true favorites from *Easy Reversible Vests* and added many new designs and sizes.

## THE PAPER FOUNDATION

The lines on each block design represent the sewing lines, and the numbers represent the piecing sequence. Using paper piecing to make blocks is quick. While a block with 5 pieces is faster to piece than a block with 15 pieces, the good news is that you can easily make a vest with just one dramatic block. So even if there are lots of pieces in the block, it still won't take long.

The block design represents the *wrong* side of the block. This is of no consequence for the symmetrical blocks with symmetrical fabric placement. However, asymmetrical blocks or asymmetrical fabric placement will result in the reverse pattern appearing on the finished side.

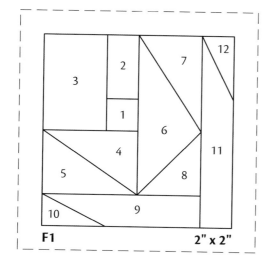

## BLOCK-FRONT DRAWINGS

The block-front illustrations in this section, which can be photocopied and used for design purposes, show how the finished blocks will appear from the fabric side. Use colored pencils to try different color schemes. Always use the block-front drawings to make your design and color selection, and note your choices on the unmarked side of the corresponding block designs.

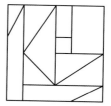

Block-front drawing showing
how the block will appear
when finished

## Cutting Lists

To make your paper piecing easy and accurate, a cutting list for the fabric sizes needed to complete each block is provided for each block design. Because you will be making just one block, or maybe a few, I've simplified the cutting lists to just a few different cut sizes. As described in "Making Paper-Pieced Blocks" on page 21, the ◺ symbol in the cutting lists indicates to cut a square and cut it once diagonally to make two half-square triangles.

| F1   3" x 3" | |
|---|---|
| **Location** | **Size to Cut** |
| 8 | 2¼" x 2¼" 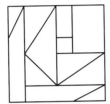 |
| 3, 4, 5, 6, 7 | 1¾" x 3¼" |
| 9, 11 | 1¼" x 3¾" |
| 1, 2, 10, 12 | 1¼" x 2¼" |

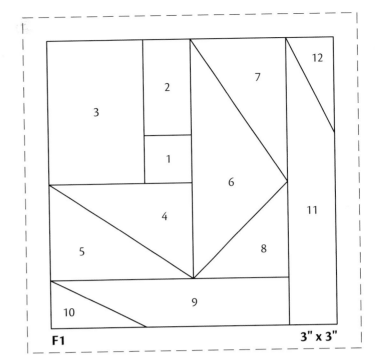

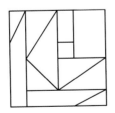

| F1   2½" x 2½" | |
|---|---|
| **Location** | **Size to Cut** |
| 8 | 2" x 2" 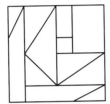 |
| 3, 4, 5, 6, 7 | 1½" x 3" |
| 9, 11 | 1¼" x 3¼" |
| 1, 2, 10, 12 | 1¼" x 2" |

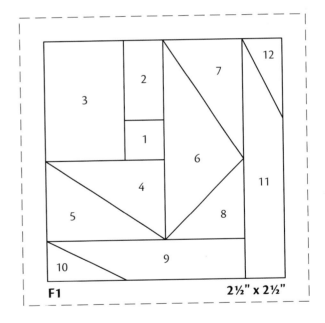

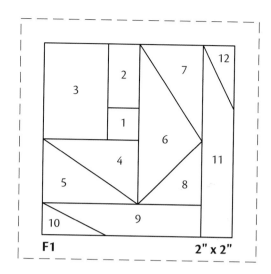

| F1   2" x 2" | |
|---|---|
| **Location** | **Size to Cut** |
| 8 | 2" x 2" ◣ |
| 3, 4, 5, 6, 7 | 1½" x 2¾" |
| 9, 11 | 1¼" x 2¾" |
| 1, 2, 10, 12 | 1¼" x 2 " |

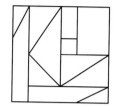

**F1**                                    **2" x 2"**

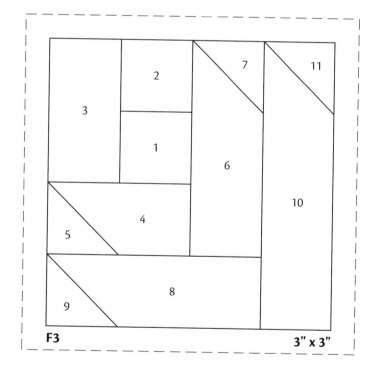

| F3   3" x 3" | |
|---|---|
| **Location** | **Size to Cut** |
| 5, 7, 9, 11 | 2" x 2" ◣ |
| 6, 8, 10 | 1½" x 3¾" |
| 3, 4 | 1½" x 2¼" |
| 1, 2 | 1½" x 1½" |

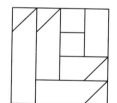

**F3**                                    **3" x 3"**

PAPER-PIECED BLOCK DESIGNS

| F3   2" x 2" | |
| --- | --- |
| **Location** | **Size to Cut** |
| 5, 7, 9, 11 | 1¾" x 1¾" ◸ |
| 6, 8, 10 | 1¼" x 2¾" |
| 3, 4 | 1¼" x 1¾" |
| 1, 2 | 1¼" x 1¼" |

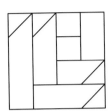

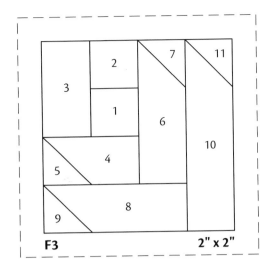

**F3** 2" x 2"

| F6   3" x 3" | |
| --- | --- |
| **Location** | **Size to Cut** |
| 10, 13, 14 | 2¼" x 2¼" ◸ |
| 7 | 2" x 3¾" |
| 3, 4, 5, 6 | 1¾" x 2¾" |
| 8, 9, 11, 12 | 1½" x 3½" |
| 1, 2 | 1½" x 1½" |

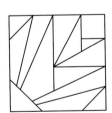

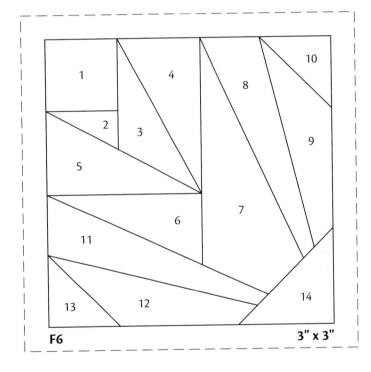

**F6** 3" x 3"

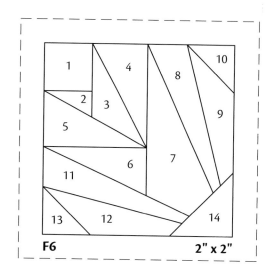

| F6   2" x 2" | |
|---|---|
| **Location** | **Size to Cut** |
| 10, 13, 14 | 2" x 2" ◺ |
| 3, 4, 5, 6, 7, 8, 9, 11, 12 | 1½" x 2¾" |
| 1, 2 | 1¼" x 1¼" |

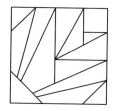

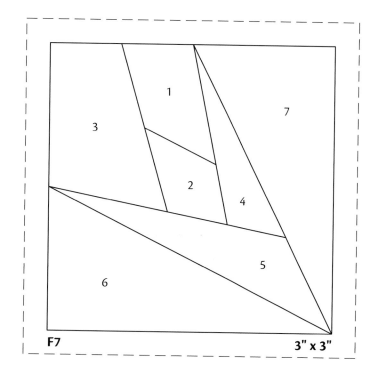

| F7   3" x 3" | |
|---|---|
| **Location** | **Size to Cut** |
| 6, 7 | 2" x 4½" |
| 1, 3 | 2" x 3" |
| 4, 5 | 1½" x 4" |
| 2 | 1½" x 2½" |

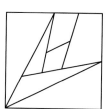

PAPER-PIECED BLOCK DESIGNS

| F7    2½" x 2½" | |
| --- | --- |
| Location | Size to Cut |
| 6, 7 | 1¾" x 4" |
| 1, 3 | 1¾" x 2½" |
| 4, 5 | 1½" x 3¾" |
| 2 | 1¼" x 1¾" |

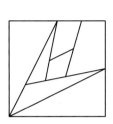

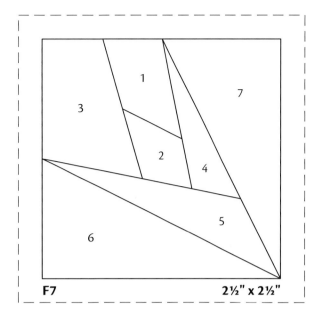

**F7**                                   **2½" x 2½"**

| F7    2" x 2" | |
| --- | --- |
| Location | Size to Cut |
| 5, 6, 7 | 1¾" x 3½" |
| 1, 2, 3, 4 | 1½" x 2¼" |

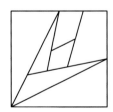

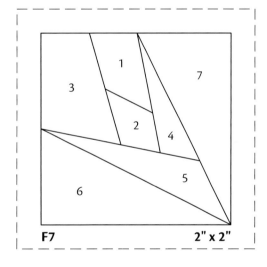

**F7**                                   **2" x 2"**

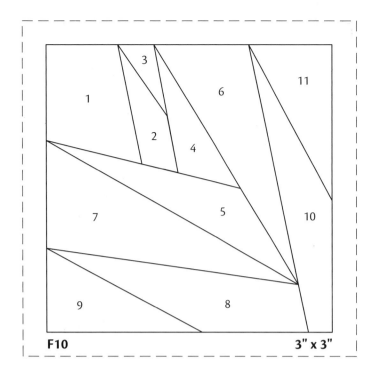

**F10**                                          **3" x 3"**

| F10   3" x 3" ||
| Location | Size to Cut |
| --- | --- |
| 1 | 2" x 2" |
| 6, 7 | 1¾" x 4" |
| 4, 5, 8, 9, 10, 11 | 1½" x 4" |
| 2, 3 | 1" x 2¼" |

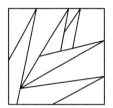

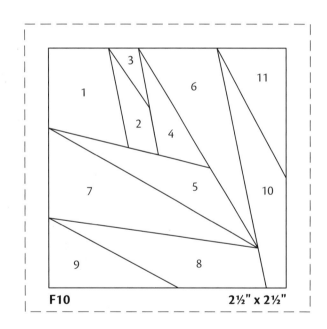

**F10**                                    **2½" x 2½"**

| F10   2½" x 2½" ||
| Location | Size to Cut |
| --- | --- |
| 1 | 1¾" x 1¾" |
| 4, 5, 6, 7, 8, 9, 10, 11 | 1½" x 3½" |
| 2, 3 | 1" x 2" |

PAPER-PIECED BLOCK DESIGNS

| F19   3" x 3" | |
| --- | --- |
| Location | Size to Cut |
| 18, 19 | 2½" x 2½" ◻ |
| 1 | 1½" x 3½" |
| 2, 3, 6, 7, 10, 11, 14, 15 | 1½" x 2½" |
| 4, 5, 8, 9, 12, 13, 16, 17 | 1¼" x 3¾" |

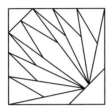

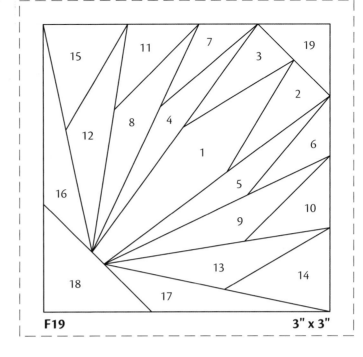

F19    3" x 3"

| G5 Variation   3" x 3" | |
| --- | --- |
| Location | Size to Cut |
| 14, 15 | 2¾" x 2¾" ◻ |
| 1 | 2¼" x 3" |
| 2, 3, 6, 7, 10, 11 | 1½" x 2" |
| 4, 5, 8, 9, 12, 13 | 1¼" x 3½" |

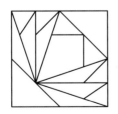

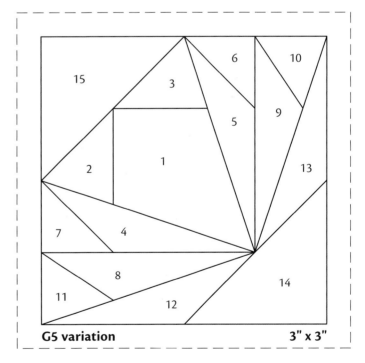

G5 variation    3" x 3"

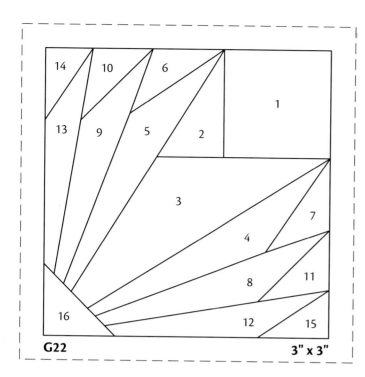

| G22  3" x 3" | |
|---|---|
| Location | Size to Cut |
| 3 | 2½" x 3½" |
| 16 | 2" x 2" ◨ |
| 1 | 2" x 2" |
| 2, 6, 7, 10, 11, 14, 15 | 1½" x 2" |
| 4, 5, 8, 9, 12, 13 | 1¼" x 4" |

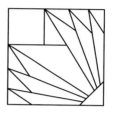

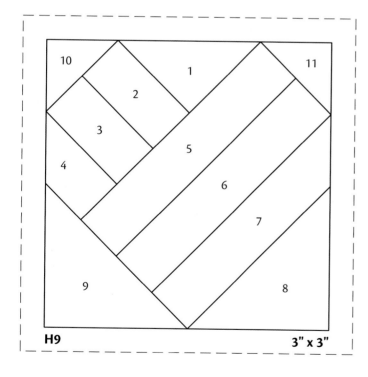

| H9  3" x 3" | |
|---|---|
| Location | Size to Cut |
| 8, 9, 10, 11 | 2¾" x 2¾" ◨ |
| 1, 2, 3, 4 | 1½" x 2¼" |
| 5, 6, 7 | 1¼" x 3½" |

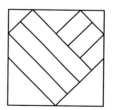

PAPER-PIECED BLOCK DESIGNS

| V1   3" x 3" | |
| --- | --- |
| Location | Size to Cut |
| 13 | 3¼" x 3¼" ◩ |
| 10, 11, 12 | 2¼" x 2¼" ◩ |
| 2, 3, 6, 7 | 1½" x 2" |
| 1, 4, 5, 8, 9 | 1½" x 3¼" |

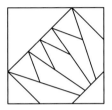

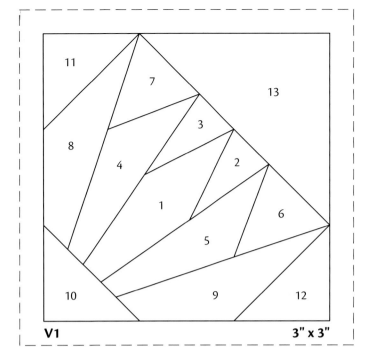

| V2   3" x 3" | |
| --- | --- |
| Location | Size to Cut |
| 1, 2 | 2" x 2" ◩ |
| 7, 8, 11, 12, 15, 16, 19, 20 | 1¾" x 1¾" ◩ |
| 3, 4 | 1½" x 2¼" |
| 5, 6, 9, 10, 13, 14, 17, 18 | 1" x 3¾" |

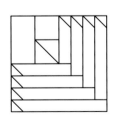

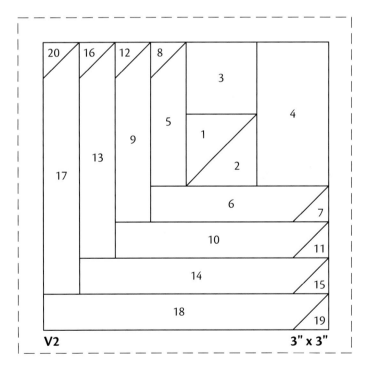

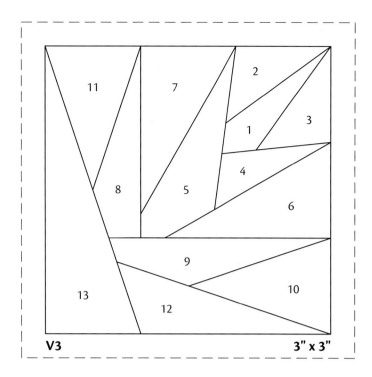

**V3**     **3" x 3"**

| V3   3" x 3" | |
|---|---|
| Location | Size to Cut |
| 13 | 1¾" x 4" |
| 10, 11 | 1¾" x 2½" |
| 5, 6, 7, 8, 9, 12 | 1½" x 3¾" |
| 1, 2, 3, 4 | 1¼" x 2½" |

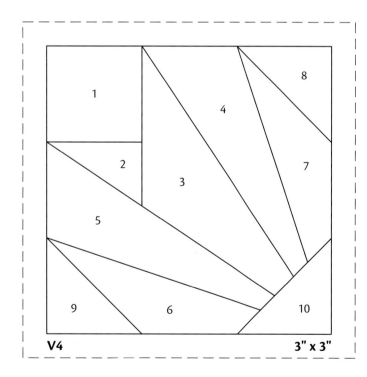

**V4**     **3" x 3"**

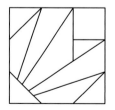

| V4   3" x 3" | |
|---|---|
| Location | Size to Cut |
| 3 | 2¼" x 3¼" |
| 8, 9, 10 | 2¼" x 2¼" ◹ |
| 1, 2 | 1¾" x 1¾" |
| 4, 5, 6, 7 | 1½" x 4" |

PAPER-PIECED BLOCK DESIGNS

| V4    2" x 2" | |
|---|---|
| Location | Size to Cut |
| 8, 9, 10 | 2" x 2" ◺ |
| 3 | 1¾" x 2½" |
| 4, 5, 6, 7 | 1¼" x 3" |
| 1, 2 | 1¼" x 1¼" |

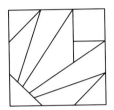

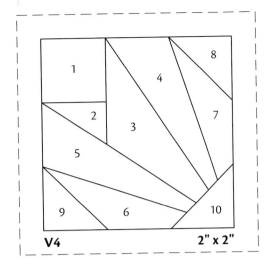

| V5    3" x 3" | |
|---|---|
| Location | Size to Cut |
| 8 | 2¼" x 2¼" ◺ |
| 3 | 2" x 2¾" |
| 1, 2, 4, 5, 6, 7 | 1¾" x 4½" |

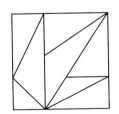

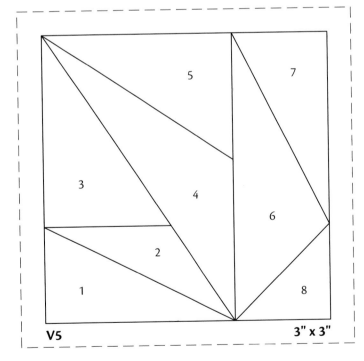

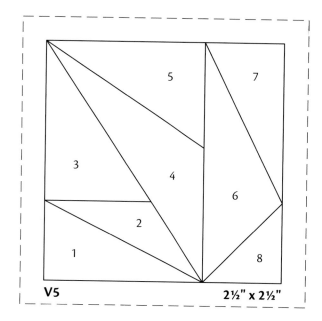

| V5    2½" x 2½" | |
|---|---|
| Location | Size to Cut |
| 8 | 2" x 2" ◻ |
| 3 | 2" x 2½" |
| 1, 2, 4, 5, 6, 7 | 1½" x 4" |

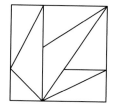

**V5**                                         **2½" x 2½"**

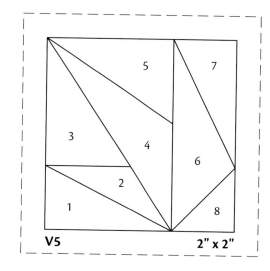

| V5    2" x 2" | |
|---|---|
| Location | Size to Cut |
| 8 | 2" x 2" ◻ |
| 3 | 1½" x 2¼" |
| 1, 2, 4, 5, 6, 7 | 1¼" x 3¼" |

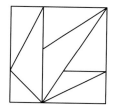

**V5**                                         **2" x 2"**

PAPER-PIECED BLOCK DESIGNS

| V6 3" x 3" | |
|---|---|
| Location | Size to Cut |
| 13 | 2" x 4½" |
| 1 | 1¾" x 3" |
| 2, 3, 12 | 1½" x 3¼" |
| 4, 5, 6, 7, 8, 9, 10, 11 | 1½" x 3" |

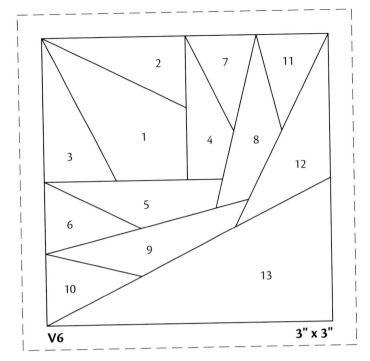

| V7 3" x 3" | |
|---|---|
| Location | Size to Cut |
| 6, 7, 12 | 2¼" x 2¼" |
| 8, 9, 10, 11 | 1¾" x 3¾" |
| 1, 2, 3, 4, 5 | 1½" x 3" |

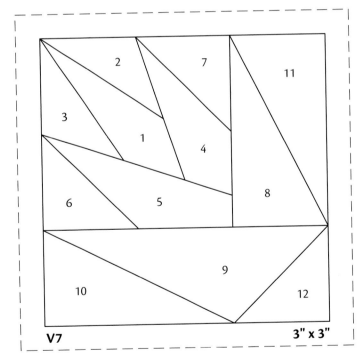

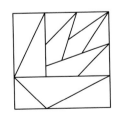

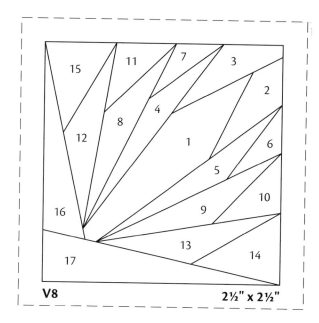

| V8    2½" x 2½" | |
|---|---|
| **Location** | **Size to Cut** |
| 1, 16, 17 | 1¼" x 3½" ◻ |
| 2, 3, 6, 7, 10, 11, 14, 15 | 1½" x 2½" |
| 4, 5, 8, 9, 12, 13 | 1¼" x 3½" |

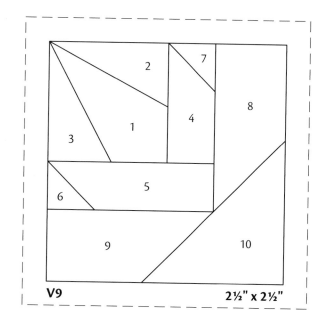

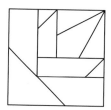

| V9    2½" x 2½" | |
|---|---|
| **Location** | **Size to Cut** |
| 10 | 2¾" x 2¾" ◻ |
| 1, 8, 9 | 1¾" x 2½" |
| 6, 7 | 1¾" x 1¾" ◻ |
| 2, 3, 4, 5 | 1¼" x 2½" |

| V10 3" x 3" | |
|---|---|
| Location | Size to Cut |
| 13, 14, 15 | 2¼" x 2¼" ◺ |
| 7, 8 | 1½" x 3½" |
| 6 | 1½" x 1¾" |
| 1, 2, 3, 4, 5, 9, 10, 11, 12 | 1¼" x 3" |

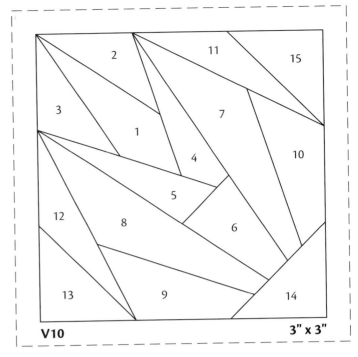

V10    3" x 3"

| V11 3" x 3" | |
|---|---|
| Location | Size to Cut |
| 1 | 3" x 3" |
| 6, 7, 8, 9 | 2¼" x 2¼" ◺ |
| 2, 3, 4, 5 | 1¼" x 3½" |

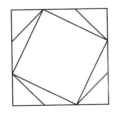

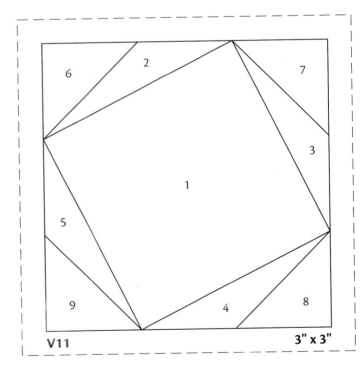

V11    3" x 3"

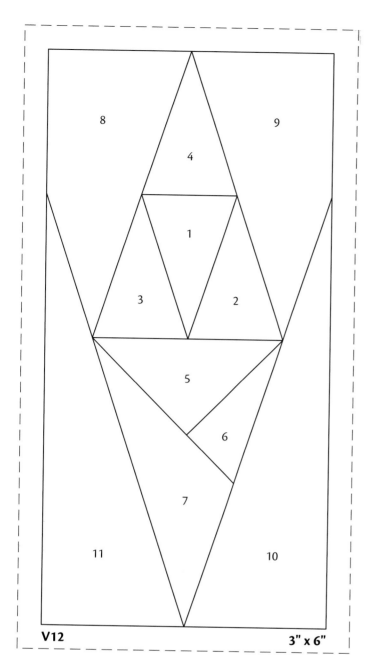

| V12   3" x 6" | |
| --- | --- |
| Location | Size to Cut |
| 10, 11 | 2¼" x 6" |
| 7, 8, 9 | 2¼" x 4" |
| 1, 2, 3, 4, 5, 6 | 1¾" x 2¾" |

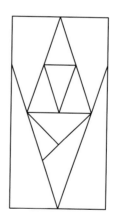

**V12**  **3" x 6"**

| V13 3" x 6" | |
|---|---|
| Location | Size to Cut |
| 6, 7 | 2½" x 5½" |
| 1, 2, 3 | 2¼" x 3¾" |
| 4, 5 | 1¾" x 6¼" |

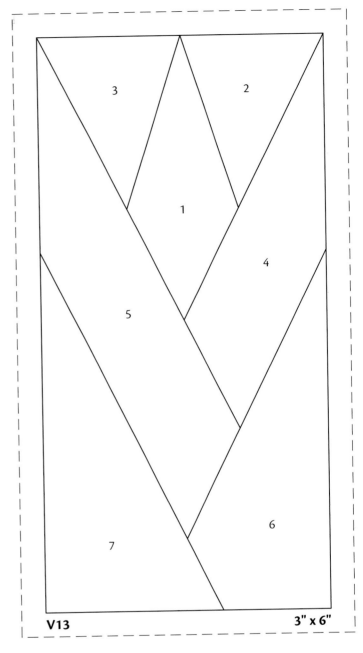

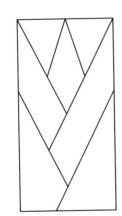

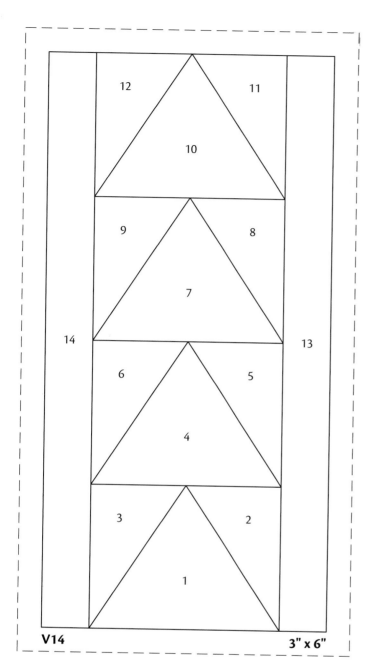

| V14  3" x 6" | |
|---|---|
| **Location** | **Size to Cut** |
| 1, 4, 7, 10 | 2¼" x 2¾" |
| 2, 3, 5, 6, 8, 9, 11, 12 | 1½" x 2¾" |
| 13, 14 | 1¼" x 6¾"* |
| *If joining two vertically, paper piece through piece #12; cut pieces #13 and #14 as 1¼" x 12¾". | |

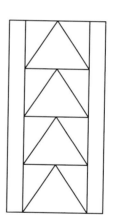

| V15  3" x 6" | |
| --- | --- |
| Location | Size to Cut |
| 7, 8, 9 | 2½" x 6" |
| 2, 3 | 2¼" x 2¼" ◺ |
| 4, 5, 6, 10, 11 | 2" x 4" |
| 1 | 1¾" x 1¾" |

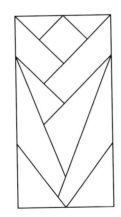

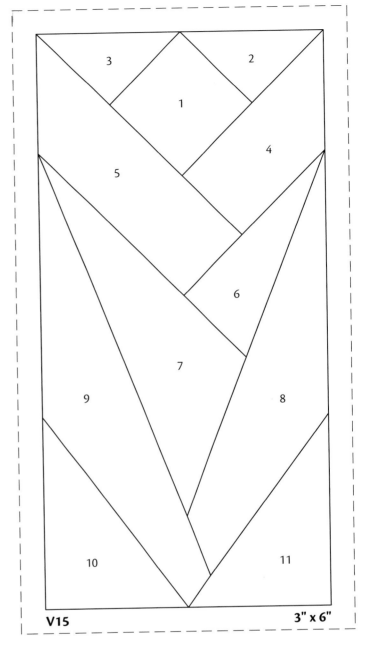

V15                                    3" x 6"

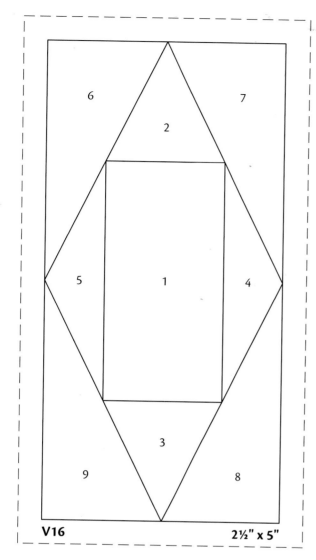

**V16**     2½" x 5"

| V16   2½" x 5" | |
|---|---|
| **Location** | **Size to Cut** |
| 1 | 2" x 3¼" |
| 2, 3 | 2" x 2" |
| 4, 5, 6, 7, 8, 9 | 2" x 4" |

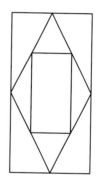

| V17   3" x 5" | |
| --- | --- |
| Location | Size to Cut |
| 8 | 2½" x 2½" |
| 4, 5 | 2¼" x 4½" |
| 6, 7, 9, 10 | 2¼" x 5" |
| 1, 2, 3 | 1½" x 2½" |

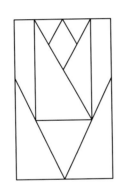

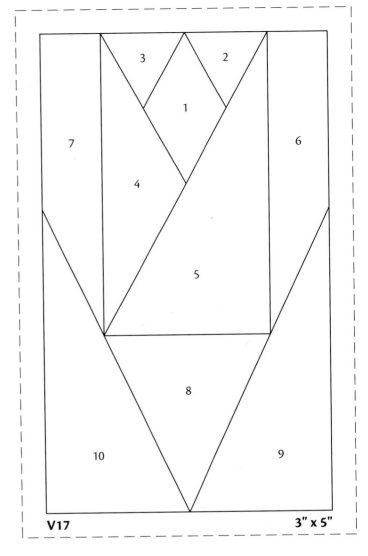

V17                                                3" x 5"

A best-selling author, celebrated teacher, and award-winning quiltmaker, Carol Doak has greatly influenced the art and craft of quiltmaking for more than a decade, both in the United States and internationally. Her accomplishments include a collection of popular books, including *300 Paper-Pieced Quilt Blocks, 50 Fabulous Paper-Pieced Stars, Show Me How to Paper Piece, Your First Quilt Book (or it should be!),* and *Easy Machine Paper Piecing.*

It's no secret that Carol has helped increase the popularity of paper piecing, her trademark technique, through her innovative designs and easy-to-follow instructions. As a teacher, Carol is known for her infectious enthusiasm for quiltmaking. She has a gift for sharing her inspiring ideas and techniques with her students in a positive and unique way.

Carol lives with her husband in Windham, New Hampshire, and is often traveling the world, sharing her love of quilting with others. Carol's newsletter and teaching schedule are available on her website at www.caroldoak.com.